MURDER AND MADNESS

The Scream by Edvard Munch.

Murder and Madness

DONALD T. LUNDE

The Portable Stanford Series

SAN FRANCISCO BOOK COMPANY, INC.

San Francisco 1976

Copyright © 1975, 1976 by Donald T. Lunde

Library of Congress Cataloging in Publication Data

Lunde, Donald T.
  Murder and madness.

  (The Portable Stanford)
  Bibliography: p.
  Includes index.
  1. Murder—United States. 2. Murder.
3. Criminal psychology. I. Title.
HV6529.L86 1976   364.1'523   75-45416
ISBN 0-913374-32-6
ISBN 0-913374-33-4 pbk.

Simon and Schuster Order Number 22287 (cloth); 22288
(paper)
Trade distribution by Simon and Schuster
A Gulf + Western Company

Printed in the United States of America
10 9 8 7 6 5 4 3 2 1

This book was published originally as a part of
THE PORTABLE STANFORD, a series of books published by the Stanford Alumni Association, Stanford, California. This edition published by ar-
rangement with the Stanford Alumni Association.

TABLE OF CONTENTS

PREFACE

I have often been asked how I first came to be involved in examining murderers and testifying in murder trials. In 1969, I was having a casual dinner conversation with a Superior Court judge who was telling me how dissatisfied he was with the quality of psychiatric experts appearing in his courtroom. I was not surprised to hear that only a few psychiatrists of the many in the San Francisco Bay Area were willing to accept court appointments to examine criminal defendants in jail, submit a written report of their findings, and make themselves available to testify at trial. The remuneration alone seemed a sufficient explanation since the courts were paying a flat fee of 40 or 50 dollars for an examination and report that might easily take four or five hours total (including travel time to and from the county jail). Furthermore, many psychiatrists have traditionally been wary of the way some lawyers try to discredit psychiatric testimony.

I made these observations to the judge, and he acknowledged he had heard them before. I also brought up the common objections voiced by psychiatrists about the archaic concepts which the law still held regarding mental illness. Judges and trial attorneys wanted psychiatrists to render and defend opinions about a defendant's "sanity." Didn't they realize that such terms as "sane," "insane," and "lunatic" disappeared from the psychiatric literature and nomenclature about 100 years ago and were meaningless to someone trained in the 20th century? Furthermore, the definition of "insanity" still in use was written about 60 years before Freud, Jung, Kraepelin, Bleuler, and the other great pioneers of modern psychiatry had begun to publish their findings and insights about mental illness.

The judge was more apologetic on this topic, it seemed, and could only point out that he did not write the law but he did have to live with it. Someday, perhaps, it would be modified, but he had more immediate concerns. He had recently been assigned a case for trial in which counsel for the defense had entered a plea of not guilty by reason of insanity. In accordance with the statutory procedure, he had appointed two *alienists* (the archaic term for psychiatrists) to examine the defendant and submit written opinions. Their reports were brief, poorly written, and of little value. One stated the defendant was sane; the other stated he was insane. The judge expressed concern that the defendant's mental state might be the critical factor for the jury to consider during the trial and that justice might be served by having available the opinion of a third psychiatrist, if he could only find one willing to take the case. It could be an interesting experience, he pointed out, for someone who had never participated in a trial before; and, of course, there was no obligation incurred in terms of any other defendants or future trials.

With some reluctance, I agreed to do it, assuming the experience would give me a better basis for stating the criticisms I had already mentioned. The case was not a highly controversial or publicized one, so I was somewhat surprised to see a number of professional-looking people in the spectator section when I testified. It seemed unlikely they could be reporters. They were not reporters, I found out later—they were lawyers, checking out the new "shrink."

In the next several weeks I received a number of phone calls and letters from lawyers and judges. A large number of criminal cases seemed to call for psychiatric input—not just murder cases but those involving sex offenses, drug addiction, child abuse, and many others. At the time, each seemed quite different from the other and I also came to appreciate how well attorneys can present their particular case as "unusually interesting." In no time at all, I found myself consulting on dozens of criminal cases of all sorts.

Murder cases generally turned out to be the most challenging and complex, particularly mass murder cases. I began to realize that my views of murder and murderers had been based on very limited data and fictionalized stereotypes which did not conform to the reality I encountered when personally examining someone charged with murder. I decided to keep particularly detailed records in murder cases, obtain all the background information I could in each case, record and transcribe my interviews when possible, and so forth.

Over a five-year period I accumulated detailed findings of my own on 40 murderers whose victims included 66 men, women, and children. In some instances I came into a case at the request of the presiding or trial judge; in other cases, at the request of attorneys for the defense or prosecution. All of these cases ultimately went to trial, and in many of them I testified as an expert witness regarding the defendant's state of mind at the time of the killing (or killings). Within a year from the time of my conversation with the judge, I was called to be a psychiatric consultant on the case of Santa Cruz mass murderer John Linley Frazier. Oddly enough, in close succession I became similarly involved in the cases of two other mass murderers in Santa Cruz—Herbert Mullin and Edmund Kemper.

Are these people mentally ill? Are they in need of treatment or punishment? In what follows I will discuss some of the myths and realities about the relationship of mental illness to murder. I have illustrated these views with case studies from my own experience. (Most of the material presented in this book about these three cases and others in which I have been involved is a matter of public record.)

I was assisted in the research phase of this book by Burt Selman, the staff of the Stanford Law Library, and especially by a Stanford medical student, Karen Train. James Jackson, defense attorney for John Linley Frazier, Herbert W. Mullin, and Edmund Kemper, and his associate, Harold Cartwright, most kindly assembled and made available to me trial transcripts and all other materials relating to the Santa Cruz mass murder trials. Martha Costain and Michele Kremen cheerfully typed the manuscript.

Throughout the months of writing I had the benefits of the support and helpful comments of my wife, Marilynn, and the enthusiastic interest and encouragement of my five sons, Monty, Chris, Glenn, Evan, and Bret, to whom this book is dedicated.

Donald T. Lunde

Stanford, California
November 1975

Credits

MURDER AND MADNESS

The Duel (Mephistopheles I) by Edvard Munch.

CHAPTER ONE

MURDER IN THE UNITED STATES

WE ARE NOW EXPERIENCING a murder epidemic that is breaking all previous records. More Americans were murdered from 1970 through 1974 than were killed during the entire Vietnam war. In 1976, one of every 10,000 American will be murdered.

The current rapid rise in the murder rate* is not an entirely new phenomenon in U.S. history. In 1900 there was approximately 1 murder per 100,000 people in the U.S. Three decades later, the murder rate had jumped almost tenfold. Then, between 1933 and 1955, it fell almost as sharply—to the lowest level since 1910: But in a mere decade since 1964 the murder rate has more than doubled. In 1974, for the first time in U.S. history, the number of murders exceeded 10 per 100,000 (see *Fig. 1*). The wide fluctuation in the murder rate raises a number of questions: What kinds of people commit murder, and why are there more murderers today than 10 years ago? Does the murder rate correlate with the state of the economy? Why do some countries, such as England, have dramatically lower murder rates than the U.S.? Is the murder rate climbing because a group of insane mass murderers have been turned loose from mental hospitals? Can anything be done to reverse the upward trend? These are questions this book will explore.

General remedies for the current crime wave are popular among politicians and voters—tougher penalties, rehabilitation programs, and in-

---

* The murder rate refers to the number of *victims* per year per 100,000 population.

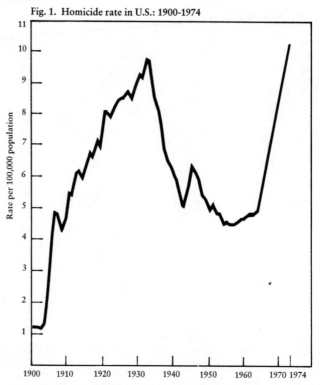

Fig. 1. Homicide rate in U.S.: 1900-1974

Source: *Homicide in the United States: 1900–1964*, National Center for Health Statistics, U.S. Public Health Service. Extended with data from annual FBI *Uniform Crime Reports*.

creased police protection, to name a few. It is falsely assumed that serious crimes—robbery, assault, rape, kidnapping, and murder—are committed by a relatively homogeneous segment of the population, "the criminal element." It is also assumed, falsely, that these people can be readily identified, and that once identified, we can stop wasting time and money on lengthy trials, appeals, and retrials—"kill them" or "cure them," and current polls seem to favor the former.

But murder has many facets, and the rapid increase in murderers is not a single, simple phenomenon. Murderers differ in many ways from those who commit less serious crimes. Few murderers fit common stereotypes; they are in fact a heterogeneous group. Rare bizarre, senseless killings receive much publicity and tend to be associated with madness, but murder is far from rare and most murders are not the work of lunatics gone berserk. Many prevailing views on murder are derived from fictional accounts from novels, movies, or television.

Murder mysteries and detective stories have created a mythology of murder that is difficult to dispel. "Whodunit" victims are often killed as part of an elaborate scheme, with a rare poison, in an intricate sequence of events arranged to make the victim's death seem accidental. In reality, most murders are committed with common weapons—guns, knives, whatever is at hand—and with little planning. Whereas fictional murderers meticulously plan their escape, making every effort to avoid detection, and often have financial motives (insurance money, a rival's business, or the like), in reality, most murderers are easily apprehended and readily confess. They seldom stand to gain financially from the killing.

At this juncture, before exploring some of the questions I have posed, I will define some key words which, for purposes of our discussion, will have a somewhat different or more specific meaning than in ordinary conversation.

The Guilty State of Mind

In making the legal determination as to whether an act of killing, homicide, is a *murder*, it is necessary to establish that the mental element, *mens rea*, which translates as the "guilty state of mind," is present when the act is committed.

Most U.S. jurisdictions have adopted the centuries-old English formulation which separates *murder* from less serious homicides by this definition: "Murder is the unlawful killing of a human being with malice aforethought." Thus, *malice* is the particular guilty state of mind that is required in establishing the crime of murder.

Malice distinguishes *murder* from lesser types of homicide (such as manslaughter, justifiable homicide, and excusable homicide). It does not necessarily require feelings of hatred or ill will toward the victim. *Express* malice is the guilty state of mind that is assumed to be present when there is proof, in the absence of provocation, of a deliberate *intent to kill* or cause serious bodily harm to the victim. The intent to kill the victim, however, need not be obvious. Malice is *implied*—that is, a killing is considered a murder—when a death results from a person's committing an "inherently dangerous act" (such as planting a bomb that kills someone in an office building, even if the bomber thought the building was unoccupied) or when a person is killed during the commission of certain felonies (such as a robbery that results in an unintentional killing). *Aforethought* does not imply deliberation or the lapse of considerable time. It simply means that the required mental state must precede rather than follow the act.

Whether a murder is first degree (punishable by death or life imprisonment) or second degree (punishable by lesser sentences—e.g., 5 years to life, with possibility of parole) depends on whether there was *premeditation and deliberation*, although killings which occur in the course of certain specified felonies (including robbery, rape, kidnapping) are automatically defined as first-degree murder and require no proof of premeditation or deliberation.

Premeditation means that the killing was considered beforehand and implies more reflection on the act than the simple intent to kill. *Deliberation* means that the act was conceived and decided upon as the result of careful thought, rather than impulse. "To constitute a deliberate and premeditated killing, the slayer must weigh and consider the question of killing, and the reasons for and against such a choice and, having in mind the consequences, he decides to and does kill."

An unlawful homicide in which malice is absent is called *manslaughter* (usually punishable by 1 to 15 years imprisonment, with judges having discretion to suspend sentence—substituting probation for incarceration). *Voluntary manslaughter* refers to an act causing death which, though unlawful, is committed in the heat of passion or is excited by a sudden quarrel that is considered sufficient provocation. In such a case, even if an intent to kill exists, the law is that malice— an essential element of murder—is absent. *Involuntary manslaughter* refers to an unintentional killing that occurs during the commission of a minor criminal act (misdemeanor)—for instance, when a trespassing hunter shoots and unintentionally kills a farmer he did not see in the distance. Deaths which occur as the result of reckless or drunken driving are also classified as manslaughter.

Justifiable homicide, which is not punishable, includes killing in self-defense or killing by police officers in the lawful performance of their duty (shooting an escaping prisoner). *Excusable homicide*, also not punishable, includes killings that result from "accident or misfortune" where there is no unlawful act of negligence involved and no unlawful intent (as when a person, not speeding or drunk, driving a car in good condition, cannot avoid hitting a child who darts in front of the car).

If a person is proven to be *insane* at the time of killing, the jury may reach a verdict of not guilty by reason of insanity. The disposition in such cases, however, is very different from those in which the verdict is simply guilty or not guilty. One significant difference is that the average confinement of a killer found *insane* is longer than for those found *guilty*.

Who Kills Whom?

Most murders in the U.S. are committed by young adults, predominantly males. More than half of all murderers are under age 35, whereas less than one-tenth are over age 50. A decade ago the average age of murderers was about 30, today it is closer to 20. The average age of female murderers is about 5 years older than that of male murderers. In recent years the percentage of women murderers has increased. Twenty-five years ago less than one-fifth of murders were committed by women; today the figure has risen to about one-fourth. Women are more likely than men to kill family members. More specifically, almost all infants who are killed are killed by their mothers. Husbands, lovers, and older children—in that order—are the next most common victims of women who kill.

Ninety-four percent of all murders are intraracial. In those cases of interracial murder, blacks are most often the victims of whites. Blacks in the U.S. murder far more often than whites, and, as most of their victims are black, the murder rate for blacks is significantly higher than for whites. (It is 10 times higher among black men than white men and 5 times higher among black women than white women.) The combined murder rate for both sexes is 8½ times higher among blacks than whites.

Less than 30 percent of all murder victims are strangers to the killer. Slightly more than 30 percent are family members or lovers. In the remaining cases, the victim is a friend, neighbor, or casual acquaintance. About one-fourth of all murders occur within the family. Half of these involve the wife killing the husband or vice versa. The other half involve parents and children or other close relatives. Murders of lovers and ex-lovers, which accounted for 7 percent of all killings in a recent survey, are closely related in motive to spouse killings—involving jealousy, quarrels, and so forth. In such killings between spouses or lovers, women are as likely to be killed as men.

Today about 30 percent of all murders are felony murders. (Whether or not there is any deliberate intent to kill, a homicide committed during certain felonies—including robbery, burglary, rape, sexual assault of a child, certain narcotics offenses, and kidnapping—is automatically considered to be a murder.) The increase in felony murders has been particularly striking in the past 10 years, even when compared with the increase in other murders. In most felony murders, the victim and murderer do not know each other. About half of all felony murders occur in connection with the crime of robbery, about one-tenth involve rape and other sex offenses, and about one-twentieth involve narcotics offenses. Almost all felony murders are committed by males.

The hallmark of a felony murder is the fact that someone died as the result of a particular felony *other than* murder. In some cases, the victim is the crime partner, killed by a nervous or inept robber in the confusion of a shoot-out.

How, When, and Where?

The usual murder weapons are far from the ingenious devices commonly found in fiction. Shooting, primarily with handguns, accounts for about two-thirds of all murders in the U.S. Knives account for another 19 percent; assault (beating, strangling) accounts for about 8 percent; and the final 7 percent involve poisoning, drowning, burning, asphyxiation with gas, or throwing the victim out a high window.

The method of killing varies somewhat with age, race, and sex. Murderers who are very young or very old use guns almost exclusively; their more limited physical strength makes them more likely to choose a weapon that is effective from a distance and requires minimal strength. Women tend to use knives or icepicks more than firearms—first, because they tend to kill in the kitchen, where knives are most accessible, and second, because fewer women than men are proficient with guns. Although stabbing accounts for only 20 percent of all murders, about 50 percent of killings by blacks involve knives. This may be partly because poor blacks can more easily afford knives than guns but, more importantly, knives are habitually carried more often by blacks than by whites. Many murders among blacks occur during an unanticipated fight in which the habitually carried knife becomes a murder weapon.

The time and place of most murders are not randomly distributed. Murder is much more common on weekends than during the week, more common at night than by day, and more frequent on or around holidays than during other times of the year. Sociologist Marvin Wolfgang of the University of Pennsylvania found, in a 1948-52 study of 588 homicides in Philadelphia, that about two-thirds of the killings occurred between 8:00 p.m. and 2:00 a.m. In a study of all homicides in Houston, Texas, between 1945 and 1949 it was found that almost one-fourth of the killings occurred on or around holidays. That people are more likely to kill during their leisure time—at night, on weekends, and during holidays—is not surprising, since it is then that they are most likely to be with potential victims (friends, relatives, and neighbors) and to be drinking. The two peak months for murder in the U.S. are July and December—when people are most likely to have holidays, vacations, and leisure time.

Murder rates in the U.S. also vary according to geographical regions. The highest murder rates are in the Southern states, the next highest in the Western states, followed by the North Central states, and the lowest in the Northeastern states (see Table 1). It is striking to note that the Southern states contain only 31 percent of the U.S. population, yet 44 percent of all U.S. murders occur in this region.

Table 1: U.S. Murder Rates by Region, per 100,000 Population (in 1973)

Northeast **7.3**	South **12.9**
New England: Conn., Maine, Mass., N.H., R.I., Vt. 3.6	South Atlantic: Del., Fla., Ga., Md., N.C., S.C., Va., W.Va. 13.4
Middle Atlantic: N.Y., N.J., Penn. 8.9	East South Central: Ala., Ky., Miss., Tenn. 12.8 West South Central: Ark., La., Okla., Texas 12.0
North Central **7.6**	**West** **7.8**
East North Central: Ill., Ind., Mich., Ohio, Wis. 8.7 West North Central: Iowa, Kansas, Minn., Mo., Nebr., N.D., S.D. 5.0	Mountain: Ariz., Colo., Idaho, Mont., Nev., N.M., Utah, Wyo. 7.4 Pacific: Alaska, Cal., Hawaii, Ore., Wash. 8.0
	United States total **9.3**

Source: FBI *Uniform Crime Reports*, 1973.

Murder rates also vary with population density. They are almost twice as high for large cities as for rural areas and suburbs. However, what is not generally known is that the higher murder rate in most large cities is the result of astronomically high rates in a few small sections of the city. For instance, it was found that two-thirds of the murders in Cleveland occurred in just three of the 42 neighborhoods of the city, where 12 percent of the population lived. Many parts of our cities are just as safe as the surrounding suburban areas—a fact often overlooked by city dwellers fleeing to the suburbs for refuge (see Table 2).

Table 2: Murder Rates and Population Density (in 1973)

Location	Murder Rate per 100,000	Percentage of Population in Locations
City	10.0	62%
Suburb	5.5	28%
Rural	6.3	10%
Total: All Areas	9.3	100%

Source: FBI *Uniform Crime Reports*, 1973.

Wherever one lives, however, the least safe location is where police protection can hardly be expected—inside a private home or apartment. More than 40 percent of all murders occur inside a home, reflecting the high incidence of murder within the family or among neighbors and

Jealousy by Edvard Munch.

friends. Within the home, by far the most common site is the bedroom, where almost one-fifth of all murders occur. More women are murdered there (usually by a husband or lover) than in any other single place. The kitchen and living room are the next most likely sites for murder in the home. The kitchen, in particular, is the most dangerous place for husbands, since a large proportion of wives who kill their husbands do so in the kitchen. Murders in the living room most often are committed with guns and typically involve neighbors, friends, or family members other than the spouse.

After the home, the next most common site for murder is the streets—which provide the setting, primarily at night, for almost one-third of all murders. Both killer and victim in a street slaying are usually male.

Of the remaining 30 percent of murders, half occur in bars and other commercial establishments. The rest take place on stairways, and in miscellaneous locations. Murders in bars typically involve two people who have been drinking together and have become progressively drunk and belligerent. Murders in other commercial establishments are most often felony murders. Murders on stairways usually occur in apartment buildings and often involve a conflict between two people who live in the building.

Victim-Precipitated Homicides

Our natural tendency is to sympathize with the victim of any crime, but particularly the murder victim, whom we tend to think of as a passive participant, struck down by a criminal's bullet. From a legal standpoint, of course, the victim is usually assumed to be innocent. After all, our common sense tells us that it is unlikely that people would go out of their way to get themselves killed. Moreover, at a practical level, it is a bit unseemly for investigators to pry into the personal life of the deceased; friends and relatives are naturally disturbed, indignant, and often uncooperative when faced with such probing. Still, in a significant number of homicides, the victim does play a contributing role in the events leading to his or her death.

Avoiding the controversial areas of unconscious death-wishes and subtly provocative behavior, sociologists have defined *victim-precipitated* (V-P) homicides as those in which the victim is the *first* to produce a weapon or resort to physical violence in a conflict that leads to a killing. Even using this narrow definition, Marvin Wolfgang found that one-fourth of the 588 homicides in his Philadelphia study were victim-precipitated. According to a study of murder in Chicago during 1968, almost two-fifths of the homicides there could be classified as victim-precipitated.

Men are the victims of murder over three times as often as women, but the incidence of male victims of V-P homicide is an astonishing 94 percent. A higher percentage of V-P homicides occur between spouses than is found in non-V-P murders. Eighty-five percent of V-P murders between spouses involve a wife killing her husband; whereas in non-V-P murders between spouses, 72 percent involve a husband killing his wife. Thus, in V-P homicides, husbands are much more likely to provoke their wives by use of force and themselves end up the fatality.

Over half of V-P murders involve stabbing. Alcohol is involved significantly more often in V-P murders than in non-V-P murders. Particularly striking is the finding that almost 70 percent of the victims have been drinking just prior to their deaths in V-P murders (versus 47 percent of victims in non-V-P murders).

V-P murder victims not only tend to be of lower socioeconomic status than the victims of non-V-P murder, but also, interestingly, tend to closely resemble the *offenders* in non-V-P cases. One striking similarity is the likelihood of a police record; for instance, in both cases such people are apt to have a previous arrest record and a record of assaults.

Some victims of V-P homicide may be indirectly committing suicide. Suicide often involves self-pity, guilt, and feelings of anger toward a loved one. The victim in a V-P homicide not only receives the ultimate punishment but also succeeds in punishing the loved one, who subsequently must bear the guilt of the killing. Such people not uncommonly have a history of unsuccessful provocations or suicide attempts and may have subconsciously anticipated, with morbid pleasure, being the recipient of more posthumous pity as a murder victim than as a suicide victim. A related phenomenon, which I will mention later in the book, is the conscious suicidal intent sometimes seen in those who commit apparently "senseless" murders in order to receive the death penalty.

The Fate of the Murderer

Few murderers, except for those consciously suicidal, consider beforehand what they will do or what might befall them after their crime. Even after they have been arrested and have had time in jail to think about their fate, most are only vaguely aware of the various verdicts possible if they go to trial and the wide range of punishments that could result.

Except for felony murderers, few killers in the U.S. make any serious attempt to escape or avoid detection. Very often the murderer remains at the scene of the killing until the police arrive. Not uncommonly, it is the killer who has called the police to report the crime. In about two-thirds of all killings, the suspect is in police custody within 24 hours.

However, if a murder is not solved within 24 to 48 hours, the chances of it ever being solved fall markedly.

Criminal homicides have the highest clearance rate of all crimes. *Clearance* means arrest of a suspect who has confessed or is linked to the crime by evidence (such as the murder weapon). In recent years, police have cleared about 80 percent of all murders, but less than 30 percent of all robberies. However, clearance does not necessarily mean conviction. A killing may be ruled justifiable homicide, for instance, or the suspect may be acquitted. In about 4 percent of murder cases in the U.S. the killer commits suicide either before arrest or before trial. (The suicide rate is significantly higher among murderers in some other countries.)

Of those persons charged with murder or voluntary manslaughter in the U.S., about 60 percent are convicted. (This rate has remained fairly constant for the past four decades.) The remaining 40 percent are not necessarily acquitted or released. Some are found guilty of a lesser offense (such as involuntary manslaughter); some are transferred to the jurisdiction of a juvenile court (generally a discretionary matter for the judge when the suspect is a minor); some are found either incompetent to stand trial or not guilty by reason of insanity and are committed to hospitals for the criminally insane.

Even prior to the 1972 U.S. Supreme Court decision prohibiting capital punishment, only a small percentage of convicted murderers were executed in the U.S.—only about five out of every 1,000 during the past 40 years. Most persons convicted of first-degree murder in the U.S. are sentenced to life imprisonment, usually with parole eligibility after a minimum number of years (e.g., 7 in California). The median time they actually serve is approximately 10½ years. For second-degree murderers, the figure is about 5 years and for persons convicted of voluntary manslaughter, about 3½ years.

The fate of the murderer in the U.S. can be summarized as follows: he or she has by far the highest probability of being arrested and convicted of all criminals in the U.S. Furthermore, the penalties for murder are the most severe in the penal system. The criminal justice system assumes that the likelihood of conviction and punishment for a particular crime acts as a deterrent. Yet, this assumption must be questioned in light of the facts about murder. Indeed, since the likelihood of conviction and punishment is significantly *less* for all other major crimes in the U.S., why is the murder rate increasing faster than the rate of other crimes? The next two chapters will examine the theories and evidence which relate violence to a variety of factors ranging from child-rearing practices to the state of the economy.

Red Virginia Creeper by Edvard Munch.

CHAPTER TWO

VIOLENCE AND SOCIAL FACTORS

THE INDIVIDUAL WHO MURDERS does not operate in a vacuum. Before delving into the psyche of individual murderers, it is important to examine social and cultural factors that may influence the incidence of violence and murder within various subcultures in the U.S.

Since the 1920s sociologists have attempted to determine whether social factors provide a basis for understanding violence in America. In addition, they have developed two major sociological theories of homicide—the *external restraint theory*, which attempts to demonstrate a relationship between murder and suicide, and the *subculture of violence theory*, which proposes a relationship between murder and a value system condoning violence.

Murder in the "Good Old Days"

Human life was never as cheap and insecure in the United States as it is at the present time and murder is decidedly more common in this country than in any other country of the world which makes the claim of being civilized.—Dr. Frederick Hoffman, quoted in *The Spectator*, March 30, 1933

During the 1920s and early 1930s, there was an upsurge in the murder rate in the U.S. similar to what we are experiencing today. Although detailed data is sparse, a few studies were done that give some sense of the social factors characterizing murderers of that time.

A study of homicide in Massachusetts from 1850 to 1924 revealed that recent immigrants, especially the illiterate and the unskilled, were the most likely to commit murder and other acts of violence. The study noted that in the 1890s, when the number of recent Irish immigrants in Boston was especially large, the Irish were disproportionately represented among those who committed murder or manslaughter. Later, in the 1920s, when Italians made up a significant proportion of the most recent immigrants to the state, they accounted for a much higher percentage of murderers than did the established population. The study showed that one-fifth of the murderers had been drinking at the time of the crime (despite Prohibition); one-fourth could not read or write; half had never been arrested before, and few were habitual criminals. The motives most commonly alleged were quarrels over a woman and other arguments or quarrels. Then, as today, the victims were primarily friends and relatives.

A study of homicide in New York State (excluding New York City) from 1921 to 1930 also showed that murder was more common among immigrants than among the native-born. Interestingly, this effect was found to diminish in one generation; the murder rate for the first generation born in the U.S. was dramatically lower than that of the foreign-born generation, particularly among Italians. An exception in this and other studies was the population of Russian Jewish immigrants, which was almost entirely unrepresented among the murderers.

In 1932, sociologist Harrington Brearley wrote *Homicide in the United States*, summarizing the findings of the various studies to date. Then, as now, the statistics showed a dramatic recent increase in the murder rate (as seen in *Fig. 1*), and it is interesting to compare the causes and the cures which were proposed at that time with those offered today. I make this comparison not to show how different conditions were 50 years ago or how naive the analysis of the problem was then. On the contrary, there were a number of similarities to the present socioeconomic situation, and many current interpretations are equally valid, and, in other cases, equally superficial and wrong.

Brearley reported an apparent correlation between wealth and the high crime rate of the U.S., as compared to other Western countries. He quoted one commentator who claimed, "Our enormous increase in wealth is in itself one of the underlying causes of the murder tendency. Temptation to murder, as well as to less violent crimes, increases on every hand." Consider the high incidence of thefts of cars, TVs, stereos, and 10-speed bikes in the U.S. today. To imply that if these luxury items were not present in such abundance, people would not be able to steal them as often, is terribly simplistic; yet, this notion of "temptation as the cause of crime" has been taken seriously enough in recent years that some cities have passed laws making it a crime to leave your keys in your car, lest you tempt a car thief.

Brearley indicted movies, magazines, books, and newspapers for publicizing and glamorizing bank robbers and gangsters. Today the same kind of indictments are still made, especially of television. Stanford psychologists Albert Bandura and Alberta Siegel have reported that violence shown on television or in movies demonstrably increases aggressive behavior in children exposed to it. Moreover, not only is general aggressiveness affected, but in some instances young people have actually imitated specific crimes seen on TV.

The high murder rate of the 1920s and 1930s was also thought to be an extension of the violence of World War I. "During the war years," Brearley stated, "parents were unable to create an aversion to slaying in the minds of their children, especially in the minds of those who were emotionally undeveloped or infantile.... One inhibition was swept away when a nation which held murder in horror suddenly broke out in sturdy anthems of praise for killers and killing." Are children raised during a war more likely to murder when they grow up? There is strong support for the theory that children exposed to violence at an impressionable age learn that killing is an acceptable way of resolving conflict.

More directly, the increase in the murder rate in the U.S. which occurred after the World Wars and Korea can be explained as a continuation of the socially condoned violence which was going on abroad. The violence is brought home to the U.S. when the soldiers return. Accordingly, the increase in the murder rate even *before* the end of the Vietnam war might be in part a result of the unique Army policy of bringing soldiers home after 1 year of combat duty, rather than leaving them abroad for the duration, as in previous wars. Obviously, the vast majority of men who kill in wartime do *not* kill in peacetime. But someone highly trained and experienced in the use of guns can be far more destructive if, for whatever reason, he does turn to murder. Several sniper murders in recent years have involved young men who received their training in the military. Lee Harvey Oswald became a marksman with a rifle in the U.S. Marine Corps.

Brearley also suggested a causal connection between an increase in the incidence of mental disorders and the increased murder rate—an idea still prevalent today. In recent years the mentally ill have been blamed for the increase in mass murders. There is some foundation for the latter notion (see Chapter 6), but no factual basis for the belief that the murder rate fluctuates with the incidence of mental illness.

Cultural patterns peculiar to certain regions of the U.S., especially the Western frontier and the South, were another aspect of Brearley's study. He noted that the practice of dueling as well as the custom of violent revenge in family feuds (the Hatfields and McCoys phenomenon) had persisted in the South far longer than in any other region and that (then, as now) the South had the highest murder rate. On the Western frontier, the notion of "might makes right" had given way to what he saw as the taming process of civilization. Yet, that the *geographical* frontier had passed signified little, for there were new frontiers of violence—the cities. Brearley observed, "Our great cities, the present hotbeds of crime, are the frontiers for a host of new Americans, offering to their released energies and stimulated wants as many immunities and opportunities as the West used to offer its bad men." Although we no longer describe our great cities as the new frontiers, many people still view them as "hotbeds of crime."

Of all the social factors Brearley cited as possible influences on the crime rate, only one was peculiar to the 1920s and early 1930s—Prohibition. But even here, a parallel exists in the 1960s and early 1970s, namely, crimes associated with another popular but prohibited drug—marijuana.

Other social factors of concern to Brearley are still familiar today: the shortcomings of the American public school system (particularly its alleged emphasis on efficiency, material success, and competition rather than cooperation); family instability and the high rate of divorce in the U.S. as compared to other countries; and the phenomenon of prejudice against ethnic and racial minorities.

In attempting to discover the underlying causes of violence, arguments about heredity and environment came to the forefront. Brearley reported great interest in genetic factors and in the assumption that some identifiable classes of people were prone to violence because of heredity or "bad genes." In the U.S. during the 1930s and earlier, some proponents of the genetic basis of crime advocated "purifying" the population by involuntary sterilization of "undesirable racial elements" and "mental defectives," the latter whom they regarded as prone to crime. In countering these arguments a report on homicide in New York State from 1921 to 1930 observed:

> ... certain investigators advocate the beautifully simple hypothesis of the existence of good races and bad races, the former not unnaturally including that group of which they consider themselves members .... The proponents of environment, differing widely in their specific views, are agreed that,

in the main, the causative factors of homicide are to be sought outside the germ plasm. They argue that in no other way could one explain the striking disparity in the homicide rates not only of different countries, but of sections of the same country. If, for example, "undesirable" racial elements are responsible for the high homicide rate of New York State, why should the ratio of murders be even higher in certain states whose white population is almost entirely native-born of Anglo-Saxon origin? Similarly, the genetic argument cannot explain the low homicide rate of Australia, a country even younger than the United States, whose early settlers were, in many cases, deported to the new continent as transgressors against the laws of their day.

As for the notion linking "mental defectives" and murder, it is interesting to note that our standards for classifying persons as "mentally defective" have changed over the past five decades. A 1925-34 study of 1,000 murderers in New Jersey reported that the average chronological age was 32.5 years, but the median *mental* age was 11.0 years. By the standards then in use about two-thirds of these murderers were supposedly mentally retarded. Similarly, a 1924-25 study of 1,916 prisoners at the Western Penitentiary of Pennsylvania reported that although most of the inmates were of normal intelligence (90-110, as measured by the Stanford-Binet IQ test), those convicted of murder or felonious assault had a median IQ of 70—considered borderline between the mentally dull and "the truly feebleminded, imbeciles and morons."

Perhaps murder was more common among the "feebleminded" during the 1920s and 1930s, but I doubt it. More recent studies indicate that the average IQ of murderers is not nearly so low. Most murderers, in fact, have average intelligence (see Chapter 7). How is this disparity to be accounted for? One explanation is that performance on the IQ test is to some extent dependent upon literacy and a knowledge of English; 50 years ago a higher proportion of murderers were illiterate and/or non-English speaking. Another possible factor is that, then as now, the illiterate and the retarded were more apt to be poor, and poor people at that time were less likely to have the services of an attorney who would provide a competent legal defense, which might lead to a conviction on a lesser charge than murder. Today, all accused murderers have a right to legal counsel and, in many cases, the public defender available at no cost to the indigent defendant is a more competent attorney than the private lawyer hired by those who can afford to do so.

Of course, the stereotype of the violent criminal who has some degree of mental deficiency, and is raised in a poor, unstable family by unloving, brutal parents, is not derived from myth. There are such people. But neither this nor any other stereotype represents the "typical murderer." Looking at murderers as a homogeneous group, we are unlikely to ever understand anything about them.

Murder in the Cities

During the 1940s and 1950s U.S. cities swelled as industrialization brought about massive migrations from farm to factory. Although the murder rate dropped for the U.S. as a whole during this period, studies showed specific areas in city after city with crime rates exceeding the national average. A 1944 study of Birmingham, Alabama, by sociologist Howard Harlan showed that a disproportionate number of killings occurred among low-income blacks living in a predominantly black downtown neighborhood. Although blacks made up only 40 percent of the total city population, he found they committed 85 percent of the murders and most of their victims (93 percent) were black. Harlan concluded, "the lower-class Negro is only a marginal participant in the society," less likely, therefore, to rely on community agencies (police, courts, etc.) for resolving disputes and personal conflicts and more likely to rely on force. "It is not difficult," Harlan continues, "to understand how the tradition of carrying weapons grows up in the lower-class Negro society. Where combat is the cultural tradition for the settlement of disputes, armed combat is the logical extension." Harlan's study of Birmingham was followed by similar studies of homicide in Houston, Cleveland, St. Louis, Baltimore, Chicago, and, of course, Wolfgang's classic study of Philadelphia. All revealed findings that were remarkably similar with regard to age, sex, race, time and place, weapons, victims, motives, and involvement of alcohol. In each city, the highest homicide rates were found in the areas with the highest unemployment and financial dependency, the highest population density and the most substandard housing, the least stability (high turnover of spouses and neighbors, many transients), the least education, and the poorest health and health care services.

In the 1960s, some social planners assumed that improving conditions in the high-crime areas of our cities—through urban renewal and the like—would lower the crime rate. If the standard of success for urban renewal was a lowering of the crime rate, and the murder rate in particular, then these programs obviously failed. But I believe the problem is that *correlations* were confused with *causes*. Using the lowering of the crime and murder rates as the criteria of success missed the point.

There never was any proof of a *causal* relationship between poor housing, poor education, poor health, etc., and the murder rate. To the extent that new housing, new schools, and new health clinics have improved living conditions, the quality of education, and the health of the population, these programs may be considered successful.

A Subculture of Violence?

Marvin Wolfgang and others who studied crimes of violence in the cities during the 1940s and 1950s found that most murders occurred among a small population subgroup whose members lived in close proximity. Wolfgang proposed a social theory to account for this phenomenon. His *subculture of violence theory* refers to a system of norms and values which expects or requires the use of violence in many social relationships and is set apart from the dominant nonviolent culture. A value system condoning violence, he suggested, is the key to understanding this subculture; the likelihood of an individual committing murder or other violent crimes is a function of the extent to which he has internalized the values of this subculture. (Excluded from this theory are carefully premeditated murders and murders by insane persons which, in most reports, make up less than 5 percent of the total number of murders.)

Wolfgang noted that young males—predominantly low-income blacks—integrated into the "subculture of violence" and segregated from the prevailing nonviolent culture, had a murder rate about 50 times higher than the rate for the general population—predominantly middle-class whites. While not claiming to be able to cite the *causes* for the existence of a subculture of violence, he did describe the salient features: insults or slurs that might be considered trivial by others are redressed by physical violence; the expectation of violence within the subculture leads its members to carry weapons in order to be prepared for "attacks" that may come at any time; the individual is more apt to interpret relatively neutral situations or everyday challenges and frustrations as threatening—and is more likely to resort to physical violence when a situation is perceived as threatening; the prevalence of weapons makes it more likely that a physical fight will end in serious injury or death; those who deviate from this value system of violence may find themselves ostracized from the subculture or may become victims of someone else's fatal aggression.

Wolfgang and his co-workers also did not attempt to explain the historical origins of this subculture, but they did suggest that if its members were integrated into the general population, the effect would be to weaken their adherence to the violent value system. There is suggestive evidence that this prediction may be true, for along with the civil rights movement of the late 1950s and 1960s and concomitant progress in racial integration, there was a decrease in the homicide rate for black males. Accompanying this decline, however, was a significant increase in their suicide rate.

The Culture of the South

It has been popular to blame racial or ethnic groups (in recent years blacks; earlier, Italians, Irish, etc.) for the values that promote a sub-culture of violence, but there is evidence that this value system is more cultural than racial or ethnic in origin. The consistently high murder rates in the Southern states cannot be ascribed to a larger black population alone, because the murder rate for Southern whites has always been higher than that for whites in other regions of the U.S. A 1949-51 study by the National Office of Vital Statistics showed a wide disparity among the murder rates for blacks in various regions of the country. The murder rate for Missouri blacks, for instance, was 4 times that for Massachusetts blacks; the rate in Texas and Florida was 2½ times that in New Jersey and Connecticut.

Two Harvard sociologists, Thomas Pettigrew and Rosalind Spier, reviewed the homicide data for 1950, concentrating on 26 states which then contained about 90 percent of the total U.S. black population. They found a wide range of murder rates for blacks in these states, ranging from a high of 39.5 per 100,000 in Texas to a low of 9.3 in Massachusetts. These facts confound those who would cling to purely racial stereotypes. They tested hypotheses in an effort to understand these differences. Differences in socioeconomic status among blacks in the various states did not correlate with the murder rate* nor did the degree of family disorganization (divorce or separation). The single prominent factor that did stand out was the culture in which the blacks had been reared: regardless of where they were currently living, blacks raised in the North had the lowest murder rates and blacks raised in the South had the highest.

Some aspects of Southern *culture* may have a bearing on the tendency toward the use of violence in resolving conflicts. Not only are murder rates higher in the South, but also rates for simple assault, involving no weapon and not resulting in death. A century ago, Horace V. Redfield spent a number of years studying patterns of homicide throughout the Northern and Southern states. His subsequent book, *Homicide, North and South*, written in 1880, contains a number of interesting

---

* The murder rates for blacks varied considerably from place to place in a pattern that did not correspond to variations in income.

observations which provide a historical perspective. Redfield gathered data from official statistics and compiled careful files. Murder rates were 10 times as high for Southern states as for Northern. New states, he noted, reflected the patterns of the home states of the settlers. Texas, for instance, which was settled largely by people from Southern states, had a substantially higher murder rate than did Minnesota, which was settled mostly by Northerners. Southerners, he found, were much more likely than Northerners to carry guns or knives, and were more likely to use them. A drunken brawl in the South, therefore, was more likely to result in a murder. But killing as the result of a quarrel was not limited to drunks, blacks, or poor whites. Homicide, Redfield observed, was also still considered an appropriate means of redressing an insult to the personal honor of a Southern gentleman, and he claimed in fact that the Western street duel had its origins in Southern tradition. Redfield also pointed out that organized group killing (by ambush or raid) occurred most frequently in the South. The Ku Klux Klan type of attack often associated with interracial violence in the South was actually made against whites as well.

Redfield felt that the Civil War was not an important causal factor explaining Southern violence because patterns of violence in the South considerably antedated the war. University of Chicago historian John Hope Franklin, in his book *The Militant South: 1800-1861*, confirms this view, describing the violent traditions of the South that were already established by the early 1800s. Long before the Civil War there was a cultural pattern in the South characterized by firearms, duels, vigilante groups, local militia, military training for youngsters, the use of military titles for status purposes, and strong interest in everything related to military training and display. Franklin points out that "The English pioneer who settled in the South could hardly be called a utopian dreamer or reformer. He had little desire to build a community radically different from that which he had left behind. Unlike his Puritan compatriot, whose dream of an entirely new order obsessed him and provided motivation for his desertion of England, the prospective Virginian and Carolinian would regard his New World venture as highly successful if he could reproduce, on a grander scale perhaps, the way of life of the mother country. The large plantation owners wished to establish estates that would retain much of the feudal spirit of a social order and way of life no longer available in Europe." The 17th-century rural English aristocracy, which, according to Franklin, "had not yet felt the full effects of the political upheavals at home or the important commercial undertakings abroad," remained their model in the 19th century. From the beginning, the Southern estates were based on extreme class differences and the availability of poor indentured white servants and later blacks. This social structure historically has been maintained by the use of harsh tactics, including violence and swift, severe punishment of troublemakers.

More important than the feudal roots of the Southern plantation may have been the fact that the South remained a frontier society longer than the North. A number of sociologists and historians have credited the Civil War with slowing, or preventing, the erosion of violent frontier traits and skills in the South while dispelling them elsewhere. In many respects the South did remain a frontier longer than the North and, then as now, the South lagged behind the rest of the country in industrialization, economic prosperity, educational level, and other factors thought to be associated with the crime rate.

Over the past decade several national surveys have shown that Southerners have a greater affinity for guns than people in other regions. Southerners are more likely to own guns than other Americans, and Southerners who do not hunt are more likely to own guns than non-hunters elsewhere. In one attitude survey, 53 percent of Southerners favored laws allowing persons to keep loaded firearms in their homes, as compared with 42 percent in the West, 35 percent in the North, and 33 percent in the Midwest. Other studies have indicated that the degree of "Southernness" of a state—as defined by the extent to which each state was settled by Southerners—correlates with the murder rate.

This discussion of traditions, attitudes, and violent crimes in the South is only intended to suggest one simple proposition: that the "subculture of violence" found in urban black ghettos in the post-World War II era was at least in part a derivative of a *regional* rather than strictly *racial* subculture, and that this subculture had its origins in the mores and traditions of the South.

Beyond this proposition, however, it should be obvious that to varying degrees the cultural aspects of Southern society that may be related to murder and other forms of violence are present throughout America. Murder in the U.S. cannot be simplistically explained as being the result of a "homicide germ" that originated in Dixie and was spread around the country by migrating Southerners.

Murder and Suicide: The External Restraint Theory

In 1917, Sigmund Freud described the psychological mechanism of *introjection*, by which he meant the internalizing of feelings toward a loved one, with the result that the emotions intended for another are directed against the self. Thus, in his paper "Mourning and Melancholia" he described the feelings of blame, anger, and self-vilification that often occur after the death of, rejection by, or departure of a loved one and that can ultimately result in suicide. Suicide, then, could be viewed as a form of murder, with the *real* intended victim (unconsciously) being the introjected, once-loved *other* person—rather than the self. Whether one accepts the pyschoanalytic view or not, murder and suicide indisputably have this much in common: the killing of a human being by a human being.

For a long time, suicide was studied by psychiatrists while murder was studied by sociologists and criminologists. But in 1949, sociologist Austin Porterfield compared the murder *and* suicide rates for 86 U.S. cities. He was somewhat startled by the finding that the homicide and suicide rates varied inversely: cities with high murder rates had low suicide rates and cities with low murder rates had high suicide rates. It was almost as if there were a fixed amount of aggression in a given population, that could take the form of either murder or suicide. Porterfield was well aware that such a theory was simplistic, but the findings were indeed thought-provoking, and he outlined a number of questions which needed further research, including:

1. How can we account for the apparent opposite tendencies of suicide and homicide rates?

2. How can the differences between Southern and non-Southern cities be explained? (He had found that in all *non*-Southern cities the suicide rate exceeded the murder rate, but in many Southern cities, the murder rate exceeded the suicide rate.)

3. Do socialization methods, particularly child-rearing practices, affect the tendency toward murder or suicide?

4. Are suicide and murder rates the highest in areas of the cities with the greatest degrees of social disorganization? (Or rather, as we have seen, with a *different* form of social *organization* and *values*?)

5. Why are women of all ages and men over 50 more apt to commit suicide than homicide? (Put in another way, why are young males most apt to commit murder?)

Partial answers to some of these questions have been offered in the preceding discussion, but the remainder of this chapter will describe the main features of subsequent attempts to answer the questions just posed.

In 1954, Andrew Henry and James Short Jr. published a sociological study, *Suicide and Homicide*. Their data supported Porterfield's finding of a negative correlation between murder and suicide rates. In addition they found that in times of economic prosperity suicide declined and homicide increased, whereas in periods of economic depression the opposite had been true. They found, too, that suicide was much more common than murder among people in higher socioeconomic groups. Combining these economic and social variables, they claimed that the homicide rate among the lower classes went up in times of prosperity, presumably because of a greater sense of frustration, whereas suicide rates among the upper classes went up during periods of economic decline, also because of a greater feeling of frustration. The question that Henry and Short attempted to answer was this: *Why does the aggression engendered by frustration lead to homicide in some people and suicide in others?* Their answer was the *external restraint theory*, which postulates that upper and lower socioeconomic groups differ in at least one important way: the lower classes are subject to more *external* restraints than are the upper classes. Because people of lower status experience frustration as coming from external sources (the boss, landlord, bureaucrat), they are more likely to blame others than themselves for their frustrations and, when sufficiently enraged, are more likely to kill someone other than themselves. Members of the upper classes, by virtue of their *relative* position in society, are more autonomous; they have greater freedom to alter the course of their affairs and experience fewer external restraints. Consequently, when things go badly, they are more apt to vent their rage on themselves. Although a lot of the facts seemed to fit into this theory, the "fit" involved some assumptions which are questionable today. Henry and Short assumed, for instance, that statistics for blacks *per se* were representative of the lower class. Since their data was collected prior to the civil rights movement and subsequent economic gains by blacks, the assumption was not, perhaps, as questionable then as now.

In any event, the external restraint theory provided a stimulus and framework for future studies, several of which examined the effects of child-rearing practices on the development of external (versus internal) restraints on aggressive behavior. It was found that children who were punished physically rather than "psychologically" (by verbal shaming, withholding of love, and the like) were most likely to express aggressive feelings toward others physically, that is, they were less likely to develop *internal* restraints. Furthermore, physical punishment was found to be more common among those groups with the highest murder rates (lower socioeconomic groups and Southerners of all social levels). This emphasis on child-rearing practices as the *source* of restraints tends to explain a finding not predicted by Henry and Short. Their theory erroneously predicted that women, because of low social status, would have higher murder than suicide rates. This was based on the assumption that women in general were subject to more external restraints than men (and therefore had low social status). However, if one looks at child-rearing practices, it is well documented that in all social classes boys are much more likely to be physically punished (and thus experience more external restraints in early childhood) than girls. This is consistent with the fact that suicide rates are much higher than murder rates for women.

Religion as a source of values and internal restraints has also been studied. The data tends to show that Jews are the most suicidal and the least homicidal. Catholics are the most homicidal and the least suicidal. (Homicide *per se* is not a mortal sin in Catholic theology; however, suicide *always* is.) Protestants fall in between Jews and Catholics for both murder and suicide.

Occupation has also been studied. An occupation representing high social status would provide more autonomy, and therefore involve fewer external restraints, according to Henry and Short. Professionals, administrators, and managers were categorized in the high status levels; clerks, salespersons, and skilled laborers were considered middle status; and unskilled laborers, low status. To the extent that occupation accurately reflects social status *and* freedom from external restraints (a proposition which some professionals and administrators might consider debatable today) the Henry and Short external restraint theory does not fit the facts: murder and suicide rates *both increase* as one goes *down* the occupational scale.

No single theory explains the cause of all violence or murder. Obviously, some social and cultural factors are important *indicators* of tendencies toward violence. But it has not been proved that such factors are either necessary or sufficient *determinants* of murderous behavior. Within any social subgroup which has a particularly high murder rate (and is assumed to be predisposed toward violence), we still find only a small minority who actually commit crimes of murder. In order to better understand this phenomenon, the next chapter will examine a number of additional factors—and whether they contribute to the murder rate.

Uninvited Guests by Edvard Munch.

CHAPTER THREE

CORRELATES OF MURDER

IT IS NOT MY INTENT to prove that any particular factors *cause* murder, but in this brief chapter I will present my own conclusions, with a minimum of irresistible editorializing, about the validity of claims that this or that factor *correlates* with the murder rate. Bear in mind that the correlations which may exist do not necessarily imply a "cure" anymore than they imply a "cause." Some possible correlates are beyond our control (such as the lunar cycle); others are perhaps within our control but it is not clear that society is prepared to exercise such control. My first topic, guns and gun controls, is the best example of the latter phenomenon.

Guns

Since 1900, more than 800,000 American civilians have been killed by gunfire. This figure exceeds the number of all military casualties in all wars from the Revolutionary War through Vietnam. In a mere two weekends in October 1974, Chicago had 26 shooting deaths, 25 of which were with handguns—more than occurred in the St. Valentine's Day Massacre of 1929. Two-thirds of all murders in the U.S. are committed with guns, 92 percent of these with handguns. Gun ownership within the U.S. is highest in the regions with the highest murder rates, and lowest in the areas with the lowest murder rates.

Obviously, the small percentage of murderers who carefully premeditate their killings and are determined to carry out their crime can find a means, whether or not guns are available. But since most homicides arise in the context of a quarrel and involve the most readily available weapon, it is worth surmising what would happen if guns were not readily available. Knives—now the second most common weapon—would presumably become the most likely weapon in the typical assault between spouses, lovers, neighbors, etc. There is good reason to believe that in such altercations knives are only one-fifth as lethal as guns, since the death rate for all victims assaulted with guns is 5 times that for those assaulted with knives.

Not all deaths by gunfire are homicides. Suicides and accidents account for more than half such deaths—50 and 12 percent respectively. Americans own more guns per capita than any other people in the world, in part because guns are so accessible in the U.S. Table 3 shows the death rate due to firearms in the U.S. compared with those of 13 countries that strictly control access to guns. (The dramatic difference between the death rate by guns in the U.S. and all other countries is not a function of population differences since the rates in all cases are rates *per* 100,000 population.)

Although a number of surveys in recent years have indicated that the majority of Americans favor stricter registration or licensing laws for guns, there have been major obstacles to the passing of gun control laws. One major problem with such laws is enforcement provisions. The Federal Gun Control Act of 1968 prohibited mail-order sales of guns and ammunition and over-the-counter sales to out-of-state residents, juveniles, convicted felons, mental defectives, mental hospital patients, and drug addicts. Even this rather modest prohibition is difficult to enforce, and people within these prohibited categories can generally purchase guns with relative ease. For instance, on the required form for purchase of a gun, mass murderer Herbert Mullin simply and falsely answered "No" to questions about a previous arrest record and previous mental hospitalization. Subsequently, he shot and killed 10 people.

Aside from the familiar arguments about the "constitutional right to bear arms," the right to protect oneself and one's household, and the legitimate uses of guns by hunters, there are enormous practical problems in attempting to impose any major form of gun control in the U.S. There are at least 50 million guns in the hands of civilians in this country; some estimates run as high as 200 million. Legislation could prohibit possession, manufacture, and sale of handguns except for law enforcement use, but how would we go about *disarming* the most heavily armed population in the world? Voluntary compliance provisions would

Table 3: Deaths Due to Firearms in Fourteen Countries (Total Number and Rate Per 100,000 Population)

Country	Homicide		Suicide		Accidents	
	Number	Rate	Number	Rate	Number	Rate
U.S. (1966)	6,855	3.5	10,407	5.3	2,558	1.3
Australia (1965)	57	0.5	331	2.9	94	0.8
Belgium (1965)	20	0.2	82	0.9	11	0.1
Canada (1966)	98	0.5	609	3.1	197	1.0
Denmark (1965)	6	0.1	48	1.0	4	0.1
England and Wales (1966)	27	0.1	173	0.4	53	0.1
France (1965)	132	0.3	879	1.8	252	0.5
German Federal Republic (1965)	78	0.1	484	0.9	89	0.2
Italy (1964)	243	0.5	370	0.7	175	0.3
Japan (1965)	16	0.0	68	0.1	78	0.1
Netherlands (1965)	5	0.0	11	0.1	4	0.0
New Zealand (1962)	4	0.2	39	1.7	6	0.3
Scotland (1963)	8	0.1	20	0.4	13	0.3
Sweden (1966)	14	0.2	192	2.5	20	0.3

Source: *Violence and the Struggle for Existence*, edited by David N. Daniels, Marshall F. Gilula, and Frank M. Ochberg. (Little, Brown and Co., Boston, 1970, p. 244.)

not motivate the millions who are opposed to gun controls or the millions who currently possess guns obtained illegally. Enforcement of non-voluntary provisions would be unworkable: the search and seizure aspect of such provisions would infringe on civil liberties and would require vast resources of manpower and money which are unavailable.

Unlike any other major country, we have carried on a domestic "mini-arms race" for generations and now face some of the problems internally that we experience on an international scale in trying to curtail armaments. The arms race aspect of gun proliferation applies to a rapidly increasing group of gun owners—those who buy guns for protection. Yet, we have already passed the point where the likelihood of personal disaster from possession of guns far exceeds the likelihood of protection. It is clear that guns increase the probability of a homicide among family members and friends. In addition, far more homeowners and family members are killed in gun accidents than are killed by burglars and robbers. Burglars make every effort to enter a house or apartment when no one is home. Protection against burglary includes a variety of approaches—burglar alarms, safes, good locks on doors, to name just a few. For those who seek protection against assault and intruders, there are now non-lethal "stun guns" available which come in a variety of sizes, including one small enough to be carried in a purse. This type of weapon fires a lead-filled leather pouch which is propelled by CO_2. Upon firing, the pouch flattens out into a pancake-shaped projectile which stuns or knocks out the intruder. There are also a variety of self-defense courses available today which offer alternatives to guns.

There is no evidence that gun control laws have had, or will have, a significant effect on the murder rate in the U.S. All states, in fact, have laws which, to varying degrees, place limitations on possession and usage of guns. There are two different approaches to gun-control legislation: (1) The first type prohibits guns to all people except those who have no criminal record *and* have a legitimate need for such a weapon, either for their line of work (private investigators, security guards), for self-defense (store owners in a high crime area), or for recreation (hunters, target shooters). Such laws are the most restrictive since only people who meet these criteria can legally purchase, possess, or carry a pistol. Only New York and Massachusetts have laws of this sort. (2) The second type of law allows all adults to purchase a pistol except for a small group of "high-risk" individuals (former mental patients, narcotics addicts, and felons). Most state laws tend toward the latter model. In fact, many states allow all people except current mental patients and felons still on parole to purchase guns.

Given the sheer number of handguns in circulation in the U.S.—with an additional 2.5 million being manufactured annually—the enforcement of strict licensing laws, even if they existed nationwide, would be virtually an impossible task. Furthermore, guns bought legally are too often resold illegally or stolen. Restrictions on the *manufacture* and importing of both handguns and ammunition would be the most effective approach to gun control, but the opposition to such restrictions in the U.S. has been overwhelming.

Alcohol and Murder

In the majority of homicides, the person who kills has been drinking beforehand. Most of these people are not alcoholics, however. We have already noted that the murder rate did not go down during Prohibition, but the only inference to be drawn from this is that Prohibition failed to curtail murder *or* drinking. In light of the higher frequency of both murder and drinking on weekends and holidays, it is easy to see why there is a *correlation* between the two, but much more difficult to say whether there is any causal connection. As there is usually a close relationship between killers and victims, it is no mystery to learn that a

Melancholy (Evening) by Edvard Munch.

large proportion of victims have been drinking as well, and in many cases the killer and the victim have been drinking *together*. A common kind of homicide I have studied involves a father and grown son drinking to excess on a holiday or a Saturday night. Other relatives are often present as well. A quarrel erupts and father or son grabs a gun, and someone is killed (sometimes a relative trying to break up the fight). The next day, when sober, the killer may have no memory of the events of the preceding night, having experienced "alcoholic amnesia."

The amount of alcohol a person drinks seems to influence the likelihood of his committing a violent crime. Persons with a urine alcohol level of .20-.29 percent (about twice the level required for conviction of drunk driving) make up the largest group of persons arrested for violent crimes.

Overall, however, the greatest number of deaths associated with drinking in the U.S. are not homicides, but deaths due to drunk driving.

The Economy

A study by Henry and Short based on data from 1929 to 1949 indicated a positive correlation between the state of the economy and the murder rate in the U.S. Overall, the murder rate tended to rise in times of relative prosperity and decrease in times of economic adversity. Yet, when the situation is evaluated more closely, this correlation is not so simple or uniform. For instance, whereas the murder rate for blacks has indeed, in the past, followed the business cycles—increasing during prosperity and decreasing during the depression and subsequent recessions—the opposite has been true for whites. In the past whites have had lower murder rates during periods of relative prosperity. There is no simple explanation for this phenomenon. Many psychologists view aggressive behavior as a response to frustration. Henry and Short theorized that blacks were less likely to prosper than whites during past economic booms and therefore were more likely to experience a sense of frustration. This heightened sense of frustration then leads to a greater likelihood of aggression, reflected in the higher murder rate. An alternative theory suggests that alcohol consumption increases in times of prosperity and that the increase in the murder rate is secondary to an increase in alcohol abuse during such periods. This theory is difficult to document because the decades when the murder rate and business cycle showed the highest correlation, the 1920s and '30s, overlapped with Prohibition. The graph of the homicide rate from the 1920s through the 1950s is strikingly similar to a graph of U.S. business prosperity, particularly the steady rise until the 1930s and the dramatic drop during the Great Depression. During the 1960s, this correlation gradually diminished so that by 1970 it had virtually disappeared. Interestingly, following the recession that began in 1973, the murder rate increased rather than decreased and the suicide rate remained relatively stable.

Suicide and Murder

The external restraint theory promulgated by Henry and Short suggested, among other things, that there is a negative correlation between suicide and murder: when the murder rate rises the suicide rate drops, and vice versa. For the entire U.S. population, this correlation has been seen during much of the 20th century, but it is not striking; there have been periods during which the correlation was reversed—most notably during the last half of the Depression era, when both murder and suicide rates decreased (see *Fig. 2*). If one considers factors of socioeconomic status, the correlations are stronger; for instance, the suicide rate for middle and upper class whites did increase during the 1930s, consistent with the theory that those subject to internal restraints are more likely to commit suicide during periods of frustration.

Fig. 2. Comparison of Homicide and Suicide rates in U.S.: 1900-1974

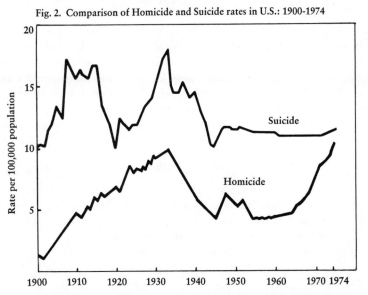

Source: Suicide rates from *Vital Statistics of the United States*, National Office of Vital Statistics, Federal Security Agency, U.S. Public Health Service. Homicide rates from same source stated in Fig. 1.

What is most striking about suicide and murder rates in the U.S. at present is not their possible correlation. For the first time in recent history, the murder rate and suicide rate are essentially equal. Until the early 1960s, the suicide rate had usually been substantially higher; from 1900 to 1960 there were about twice as many suicides as homicides in the U.S.—all of which is consistent with the theory that Americans are decreasingly subject to internal restraints.

Capital Punishment and Murder

There is no significant correlation, either positive or negative, between the threat of the death penalty and the homicide rate in the U.S. Most murders are impulsive acts that arise out of a situation in which the assailant reacts quickly, without reflecting upon possible long-term consequences. Of the 40 murderers I have examined, only two had given any thought to the possibility of the death penalty, and in both these cases the defendants were depressed, suicidal, and *wanted* the death penalty (neither received it). Also, it should be remembered that the death penalty has been administered in only a small percentage of murder cases (less than half of 1 percent in modern times), and then only after considerable delay. To the extent that punishment deters crime, it is thought to be a function of the swiftness and certainty of punishment, rather than the severity. Although criminologists tend to agree with this proposition, it should be noted that it is based in large measure on the findings of experimental psychologists who were studying the modification of behavior of non-criminal subjects in a laboratory situation. Furthermore, the death penalty as a punishment does not "deter" the offender, it eliminates him. Unlike a fine or imprisonment, it is obviously not intended to modify the future behavior of the convicted murderer. Some advocates of capital punishment argue that it deters non-offenders from becoming offenders. This argument can ultimately be neither proved nor disproved.

Youth and Murder

A 1974 report from the National Center for Health Statistics attributed the rising murder rate to the increased proportion of young people (15-29 years old) in the population. Although young people presently have the highest murder rate, the proportion of youth *per se* is not an explanation, since American youth have not always been so murderous. A recent study in Canada showed no correlation at all between the murder rate and the proportion of young people in the different provinces.

Chromosomes

Since the late 1960s there has been considerable research on the relationship of male sex hormones to aggressive behavior. Since these hormones are present because of the Y sex chromosome, there has been speculation that persons with an abnormal extra Y chromosome (the "XYY syndrome") would tend to be unusually aggressive. Some studies have suggested a higher incidence of violent crimes among XYY persons. However, the most that can be said is that there is a higher percentage of XYY individuals in prisons and maximum security hospitals for the criminally insane, but most of these persons did not commit murder and many did not commit violent crimes.

A controversial study, which began in 1968 and is still in progress at Harvard Medical School, suggests that XYY boys are more impulsive than XY boys. However, the data is not overwhelming. Some news reports about the "criminal chromosome" in fact have been erroneous; for instance, it was falsely rumored that Richard Speck, killer of eight student nurses in Chicago, had XYY chromosomes. Mass murderer Edmund Kemper fit one proposed description of the XYY—unusually tall, above average intelligence, and unusually violent. Yet tests performed at Stanford Medical Center showed he had normal chromosomes. To date, no significant correlation has been demonstrated between chromosome defects and murder.

Mental Illness

There is a slight *negative* correlation between mental illness and murder. That is, the percentage of murderers among former mental hospital patients is *lower* than that among the general population of the U.S. This is in contrast to the implication of headlines which read, "Murder Suspect Is Ex-Mental Patient." Most forms of mental illness do not predispose a person to crimes of violence. As we shall see in Chapter 7, certain personality traits and psychological profiles are common to certain kinds of murderers, but these characteristics are not synonymous with mental illness. Most murderers do not have a history of mental illness or psychiatric treatment. On the other hand, among the small proportion of murderers who are mentally ill, the single most common disorder is paranoid schizophrenia. The characteristics of this disorder are described in Chapter 6 in the case history of mass murderer Herbert W. Mullin.

The Lunar Cycle

Man's long fascination with the moon has produced many myths, including the notion that mental illness ("lunacy") is somehow related to the workings of the moon. Surprisingly, the murder rate has been found to correlate slightly with the lunar cycle, according to a 1956-70 study conducted in Florida. It was reported that the highest number of murders tended to occur at full moon, with a second peak just after the new moon. The lowest number of murders tended to occur at the dark phase of the lunar cycle. Some scientists have speculated about *biological tides* which might account for these apparent variations in human behavior. The term "biological tides" was coined to refer to supposed fluctuations in the distribution of body fluids caused by the moon, analogous to the cyclic variations of oceanic tides. However, the gravitational effects of the moon on humans are infinitesimal. A simpler explanation is that any reported effects of the moon on the murder rate are actually related to the variations in moonlight during the lunar cycle. Murders at night do occur somewhat more often when there is bright moonlight.

Magnetic Fluctuations

Magnetism has also been associated with the murder rate. The major cause of geomagnetic fluctuations on earth is the sun. Solar eruptions cause changes in the earth's magnetic field, and studies of solar-related geomagnetic activity show that it tends to follow a 27-day cycle (equal to the length of time in which the sun rotates once relative to the earth), and that it also shows a pattern of weekly fluctuation as well as a long-term (11-year) cycle. Some reliable scientists have reported a slight correlation between magnetic fluctuations and murder. However, *any* phenomenon that fluctuates on a weekly basis will show a correlation with the murder rate because the murder rate fluctuates on a weekly basis, peaking on weekends. This is a good example of a correlation which does *not* imply a causality but simply a tendency to fluctuate in a similar pattern.

Weather

There is a slight positive correlation between good visibility and murder. (This is consistent with the findings regarding the lunar cycle.) For any *given location*, however, there is no significant correlation between murder and weather variables such as temperature, humidity, barometric pressure, rain, or wind.

Seasonal fluctuations in the murder rate are minimal and probably reflect holidays and vacations rather than any climatic effect. (By contrast, suicides do show a seasonal variation, with the highest rate occurring in the spring.)

Latitude

In the U.S., the murder rates increase with decreasing latitude—that is, as one moves southward—which is consistent with the concept of a regional subculture of violence. It is interesting that those countries with higher murder rates than the U.S. (such as Colombia, Mexico, South Africa, Guatemala and Nicaragua) lie closer to the equator. Still, I can think of no plausible theory which would support the notion that this correlation indicates a causal relationship between latitude (and associated weather) and the murder rate.

The wide range of murder rates from country to country is most likely a function of cultural differences and differences in factors described earlier in this chapter, such as access to guns. In the next chapter, I will describe some of the known variations in murderous behavior in other societies.

Anxiety by Edvard Munch.

CHAPTER FOUR

MURDER IN OTHER COUNTRIES

IT IS A SOMEWHAT PECULIARLY American trait to publish unflattering information about criminal activity in our society and to be genuinely surprised when we learn that other countries do not do likewise. In some democratic European nations as well as a variety of communist countries and right-wing totalitarian regimes, political censorship impedes the gathering and/or dissemination of such information. In other cases the lack of information can be attributed to inadequate or incompetent record-keeping. Many countries which regularly publish mortality figures categorized by cause of death combine "homicide and acts of war" as a single category, making it difficult to determine the true murder rate. Nonetheless, from the data available, interesting comparisons can be made.

Murder Rates Around the Globe

Most countries, except for the Soviet Union and China, report murder rates to the United Nations. These figures indicate that at least 80 percent have lower murder rates than the U.S. Although many countries have experienced increased murder rates during the past decade, the U.S. has experienced one of the most dramatic—about 100 percent. Few countries in modern times have reported murder rates exceeding the present U.S. rate of over 10 per 100,000. Exceptions include Burma,

South Africa, Nicaragua, Colombia, Guatemala, and Mexico. For the past 50 years, Mexico has had an average yearly murder rate exceeding 30 per 100,000, one of the highest in the world. During the same period, by contrast, our northern neighbor, Canada, has had an average yearly murder rate of well under 2 per 100,000. In the middle ground was the U.S.—at almost 8 per 100,000.

Murder rates for American blacks are several times higher than those for tribal African blacks. For that matter, the murder rate for U.S. whites also exceeds that of some black African tribal societies. Cross-culturally, the murder rate does not appear to be racially linked. There is also no strong correlation between murder rates and the level of cultural and industrial development. For instance, a study of 40 nonliterate societies from Africa to the South Pacific showed as wide a range in murder rates as is seen among literate industrialized societies.

Murder and Suicide

The inverse relationship between murder and suicide, discussed in Chapter 2, has been observed in other industrialized societies (e.g., Denmark, Finland, and Sweden) as well as in the U.S. However, this relationship is not apparent in primitive societies. Some tribes have high rates for both murder and suicide, others have low rates for both.

The political, social, and economic changes brought on in the 1800s by the Industrial Revolution seemed to create a tendency toward suicide rather than murder; this tendency was seen particularly in Protestant countries. In the 19th century, England and Prussia had relatively high suicide rates and low murder rates, and all of the Scandinavian countries (except Norway) had and still have high suicide rates. The suicide rate gradually increased and the murder rate fell in France during this time, but in most other Catholic countries, this trend was not seen. In 19th century Europe, Spain, Ireland, and Italy had the lowest suicide rates and the highest murder rates.

More recent studies do not indicate any clear cross-cultural trends toward suicide rather than murder as developing countries industrialize. However, a tendency toward murder rather than suicide still exists in Catholic countries today. In the 20th century Mexico and Guatemala, in particular, have two of the highest annual murder rates and lowest suicide rates of any countries in the world. Religion and cultural traditions appear to play a far more important role than does industrialization in influencing any propensity toward either suicide or murder. For instance, Japan, the most industrialized nation in Asia, has a very high suicide rate and a relatively low murder rate. The Japanese tradition of *hara-kiri* existed long before the 20th century and fostered a condoning rather than condemning attitude toward suicide that is still present today.

In the context of Henry and Short's theory of external restraint one might argue that both Japanese tradition and Protestant theology emphasize internal restraints and therefore encourage self-blame. Furthermore, they lack the mechanism of the Catholic confession and absolution which can provide relief from the self-punishing burden of guilt that may lead to suicide. The Catholic Church, on the other hand, may be said to utilize external restraints to a greater extent, particularly in those Catholic countries where government, churches, and schools are intermixed. A greater reliance on external restraints coupled with a strong condemnation of suicide may account for the high murder-versus-suicide ratios observed in Catholic countries. (Suicide is the only mortal sin which precludes the possibility of confession and absolution.)

Tradition and religion may influence the *relative* incidence of murder and suicide in a given society, but other factors such as the availability of lethal weapons, level of alcohol consumption, or conditions which foster a subculture of violence may be of critical importance in understanding the *actual* murder rate in a given society. For instance, in certain isolated areas of Italy, a long-standing tradition of vendetta exists which is *local* rather than national in its origins and practice.

The remainder of this chapter will compare and contrast the *general patterns* of murderous behavior in the U.S. with that of three other societies.

England

In many respects, England and the U.S. seem very similar. Our criminal justice system is patterned after the English system: the underlying concepts are the same and many of our criminal laws were copied verbatim from English law. However, throughout the 20th century, the U.S. murder rate has been almost *20 times* as high as England's. The murder rate in England has fluctuated only very slightly (within a range of 3.6 to 5.0 per *million* population over the past 20 years). During an entire *half century* (1900-50) there were about 7,500 murders in England. There were well over twice that many murders during a single year (1974) in the U.S.!

In recent years there has been a steady increase in violent assaults in England, but very little increase in the murder rate. In part, this must be due to the scarcity of handguns in England. Whereas there are approximately 13,500 handguns per 100,000 people in the U.S., there are fewer than 500 handguns per 100,000 population in England. Both possession and use of these weapons are tightly controlled in England even for police, and unlike the U.S., this control has existed for hundreds of years. British gun laws follow the "restrictive" model described in the previous chapter, in which handguns are prohibited to all except highly selective groups of people who require guns for law enforcement or legitimate recreational purposes. This scarcity of guns probably accounts for the rare occurrence of felony-murder in England. Robbery is not uncommon, but armed robbery is, compared to the U.S. Recall, by contrast, that murder in the course of robbery and other felonies accounts for almost 30 percent of all murders in the U.S.

The association of madness with murder is much more common in England. Not only are one-fourth of English murderers found legally insane (versus about 2-3 percent in the U.S.), another 30 percent commit suicide immediately after committing murder (versus about 4 percent in the U.S.). As there is strong evidence that some of these persons are also insane, the proportion of insane murderers is 15 or 20 times as high as in the U.S. Since the incidence of mental illness itself is not significantly different in England, one must attribute the striking difference in the number of insane murderers to other factors. In part, it may be due to the higher incidence of felony-murders in the U.S., since the offenders in this category are least likely to be insane by legal standards. In addition, there appears to be a much greater reluctance in the U.S. than in England for jurors to find a mentally ill offender legally insane. In some cases in the U.S., this results from misleading pre-trial publicity (which is forbidden in England) and mistaken assumptions about the meaning of an insanity verdict—for instance, that the killer will be set free if found insane (see Chapter 8).

Even more often than in the U.S., murderers in England are closely related to their victims (about half of all cases). The most common methods of killing in England are stabbing, asphyxiation, and striking with a blunt instrument. Shooting and poisoning are the least common methods. As in the U.S., murder is predominantly a male activity.

The Soviet Union

The Soviet government does not report the total number of murders that occur per year in the U.S.S.R., but it does release data about the *pattern* of murder, in terms of percentages. Releasing actual raw data presumably might be politically and ideologically embarrassing, since crime is supposed to disappear in a Marxist state.

Criminal behavior associated with drinking has been a subject of great concern in Russia for many years. It has been reported that at least 75 percent of homicides in the U.S.S.R. are committed by drunken offenders. Murder by a mentally ill person, however, was *never* mentioned until very recently (1974), and little is known about the association of madness with murder in the U.S.S.R.

Murder is much less common among women in the Soviet Union than in the U.S. (about 5 percent of murderers in the U.S.S.R. are female versus about 25 percent in the U.S.). The only data available for a Soviet city indicates that almost one-half of the murder *victims* in Moscow are women (versus one-fourth in Wolfgang's study of Philadelphia homicides). However, on a nationwide basis, the proportion of female murder victims in the U.S.S.R. is similar to that in the U.S.—about one out of five. Approximately 80 percent of homicide victims are known by the murderer. As in most countries, the killing of strangers is the least common type of homicide. Over 60 percent of murders in Moscow occur in homes (versus 51 percent in Philadelphia).

Firearms are not as plentiful in the Soviet Union as in the U.S.; they are particularly scarce in Soviet cities. In a study of Moscow, only 4 percent of murders involved guns, whereas in a study of three rural provinces, one-third of murders involved guns. This difference can be traced to the availability of rifles for hunting purposes in the rural areas, versus the scarcity of firearms in the cities, where the possession of handguns is outlawed to the general public. The most common means of killing in the U.S.S.R. are stabbing, beating with a blunt instrument, and physical assault—in that order. Except for a higher incidence of murder involving so-called "hooligan motives" (not clearly defined, but implies disorderly conduct involving drunkenness), reported motives in general are similar to those in the U.S. and include revenge, jealousy, profit, and killing in the course of a sex crime.

A study of attempted murders revealed that 95 percent of the attempted murders in the Soviet Union failed due to the victim's escape, a missed shot, or the victim's failing to die from injuries intended to inflict death. In only 5 percent of the Soviet cases was the attempted murder prevented by intervention of a private citizen or police officer. Primarily, these figures reflect the fact that most murders and attempted murders occur within the home. However, in almost a third of all murders which occurred on the street in Moscow a contributing factor cited was "non-interference by eyewitnesses." Despite the Soviet emphasis on citizen responsibility, the Russian city-dweller, like his U.S. counterpart, seems to prefer not to get involved.

Hong Kong

The People's Republic of China does not report *any* data on murder, apparently for the same reasons as the Soviet Union (political and ideological). In fact, the only detailed data for murder among a Chinese

Funeral March by Edvard Munch.

population is from Hong Kong. Although it is a British colony, Hong Kong shows differences in the pattern of murder which reflect the Chinese culture as well as factors peculiar to Hong Kong (such as opiate addiction and a large immigrant population).

The most common means of inflicting death in Hong Kong is not stabbing, as in England and the Soviet Union, or shooting, as in the U.S. The majority of murders involve cutting, usually with a chopper of the sort available in every Chinese kitchen. (Interestingly, the Chinese word for "kill" means killing with a cutting weapon—which historically referred to beheading with a sword.) Until about 1960, the murder rate for Hong Kong was somewhat higher than that for England, but substantially lower than that for the U.S. Since 1961, the rate has steadily increased. This may be related to the large influx of refugees from mainland China in the late 1950s and early 1960s.

Hong Kong has essentially the same system of criminal laws as England and the United States and the same legal criteria for sanity. By these criteria about 7 percent of murderers in Hong Kong are insane (versus 25 percent in England, 2-3 percent in the U.S.). Additionally, 5 percent of murderers in Hong Kong commit suicide (versus about 30 percent in England, 3-4 percent in the U.S.).

A 1961-71 study of *all* homicides in Hong Kong showed that 20 percent of the insane murderers were women, but interestingly, *none* of the *sane* murderers was female. This is in sharp contrast to the U.S. (25 percent), England (15 percent), and the U.S.S.R. (5 percent). The average age of the sane murderers was 25, all of whom were ethnic Chinese males. The insane murderers were generally older, and among this group, the most common diagnosis was paranoid schizophrenia (as in the U.S. and England). Other diagnoses, such as depressive psychosis, were less common but appeared in about the same proportion as in the U.S. and England.

Motives among the sane murderers included quarrel, revenge, jealousy, profit, and killing in the course of a sex crime or attempting to avoid arrest. In contrast to the U.S.S.R. and U.S., alcohol consumption was rarely involved in murders among this Chinese population. On the other hand, almost 10 percent of the sane murderers were narcotics addicts.

The victims of the insane murderers were relatives in half of the cases, and the victims of the female insane murderers were usually infants or children. In all cases where sane murderers killed a relative, the victim was the wife. The intrafamilial aspect of murder seems to be common to all cultures.

Mass murders were also reported, and multiple victims were twice as common among the insane group of murderers. The phenomenon of mass murder—and its greater likelihood among the seriously mentally ill—is also common to all cultures and all periods of history.

My own interest in the psychology of murderers grew out of my personal experience as consultant to attorneys for a series of mentally ill mass murderers. The next two chapters explore the individual psychology of mass murderers, as seen from a presentation of case histories of three mass murderers, in whose trials I was closely involved. These case histories demonstrate the less common but most obvious connection between murder and madness—and provide a view into how the mental health care and the penal systems "treat" mentally disturbed criminals.

In the Man's Brain by Edvard Munch.

CHAPTER FIVE

STUDIES OF THE MASS MURDERER

MOST MURDER INVOLVES the taking of a single human life, and usually the victim is a relative or is at least known to the killer. Abhorrent as the crime is, it seems comprehensible, at least at some level: the classic love triangle is familiar enough to most people so that, while not condoning the crime, a person at least feels he or she knows how such things happen. Unlike the love triangle or the barroom brawl, the mass murder seems inexplicable. In many respects it is.

In common usage of the term, *mass murderer* is applied to someone who kills a number of people, usually for no apparent reason or for an apparent but perverse (often sexual) reason. Psychiatric and legal literature sometimes make a distinction between *mass murder* and *serial murder*, with *mass murder* referring to a crime in which a number of victims are killed, usually by one person in a single episode—for instance, the killing of eight student nurses by Richard Speck in Chicago in 1966—and *serial murder* referring to a number of murders by a single person over a period of months—or, occasionally, years. Each killing is usually a discrete episode, but there is usually a common motive, method, and/or type of victim; for instance, the series of murders of prostitutes in England attributed to Jack the Ripper.

Mass Murderers Versus Single Murderers

Mass murderers are almost always insane, and they differ in many other respects from those who kill only one person. In the U.S., mass murderers are almost always white males, whereas single murders are not uncommonly committed by blacks and by women. In my own study of 40 murderers, the only female who killed more than one victim was an 18-year-old who killed two children that she was babysitting. Whereas in single killings the murderer is often intoxicated, alcohol is rarely a factor in mass murders nor is intoxication with any other drugs.

The most important contrast between mass murderers and murderers of a single person is the difference in their relationships to the victims. Those who kill only one person usually have either a specific *personal* relationship to the victim (spouse, child, drinking companion) or *no relationship at all* (liquor store attendant, bank employee or patron killed in the course of an armed robbery). The mass murderer's relationship to his victims falls somewhere in between these two possibilities. Although the mass murderer usually does not know his victims well, if at all, their selection is not random or coincidental. He often perceives his victims as having certain attributes which torment him. The victims, however, are unaware of their psychological or symbolic significance to the killer, although the mass murderer sometimes assumes, wrongly, that they *are* aware of their desirability for his sexual predilections or their place in his delusional scheme. For instance, he may believe they have received "telepathic" messages from some divine agent informing them of the killer's mission or warning them of their fate if they continue certain "evil" practices.

Most mass murderers can be characterized as one of two distinctly different types: they are usually either paranoid schizophrenics or sexual sadists. *Paranoid schizophrenia* is a psychosis characterized by hallucinations ("hearing voices" in most cases), delusions of grandiosity or persecution, bizarre religious ideas (often highly personalized), and a suspicious, hostile, aggressive manner. *Sexual sadism* in its extreme form is a deviation characterized by torture and/or killing and mutilation of other persons in order to achieve sexual gratification.

The following case histories demonstrate the kind of disordered thinking and emotions seen in each of these types of mass murderer. I have included background information obtained from my psychiatric examinations as consultant to the defense counsel in order to provide the reader with a sense of what kind of lives these men led prior to becoming killers. Childhood experiences were no doubt of some significance in shaping their ultimately distorted views of the world, but I do not wish to imply that these early emotional traumas *caused* their later problems. The fact is that we do not *know* the precise causes of these psychotic mentalities. Nonetheless, psychiatry can offer insights as to what factors are likely to aggravate or alleviate these conditions before they erupt in murderous behavior. In later chapters of this book I will discuss how psychiatry and the law could more effectively deal with the individuals I am about to describe. These cases show how limited and inadequate our present procedures and institutions are.

Case Study: A Paranoid Schizophrenic, John Frazier

On October 19, 1970, John Linley Frazier killed a prominent eye surgeon, Dr. Victor M. Ohta, his wife, their two young sons, and the doctor's secretary. Frazier blindfolded, bound, and shot each one and threw the bodies into the swimming pool of the Ohta's dramatic $300,-000 flagstone home, located on a hilltop overlooking a tree-studded canyon with the city of Santa Cruz and the Pacific Ocean in the distance. The bodies were discovered shortly after 8:00 p.m. when firemen responded to a report that the Ohta house was on fire. They were delayed briefly in reaching the house because Dr. Ohta's red Rolls-Royce sedan blocked the driveway. Under the windshield wiper was a bizarre typewritten note which read:

> halloween....1970
> today world war 3 will begin as brought to you by the pepole of the free universe.
> From this day forward any one and ?/or company of persons who missuses the natural environment or destroys same will suffer the penalty of death by the people of the free universe.
> I and my comrads from this day forth will fight until death or freedom, against anything or anyone who dose not support natural life on this planet, materalisum must die or man-kind will.
> KNIGHT OF WANDS
> KNIGHT OF CUPS
> KNIGHT OF PENTICLES
> KNIGHT OF SWORDS

Down the hillside from the Ohta home was a grove of redwood trees, and beyond that a collection of ramshackle sheds, a house trailer, and a dry gulch filled with the stripped and rusted hulks of old cars. A woman named Pat Pascal lived in the house trailer. Across the gulch was a dilapidated cow shed, which could be reached via a rickety bridge consisting of loose boards resting precariously on some cables. During the four months preceding the murders, Mrs. Pascal's son had intermittently occupied the cow shed. His name was John Linley Frazier. He was 24 and was separated from his wife.

John Frazier's own parents had separated when he was two. By the time he was five his mother had placed him in a foster home because she was unable to both support herself and care for him. During his adolescence he frequently got into trouble—at school (for truancy), at home (for running away), and on at least one occasion with the police (for theft). For each of these offenses he was committed to one of the California Youth Authority facilities, which ranged from institutions that were prison-like to others more similar to a school. Although he spent many months in various facilities, he was not highly motivated to participate in the educational and vocational training programs available, and he was not identified as needing psychiatric treatment. The latter is not surprising since psychiatric services are very limited in these facilities, and only the obviously "crazy" youth is likely to receive treatment. Furthermore, the blatant symptoms of paranoid schizophrenia rarely appear before the twenties, and were not apparent when Frazier was a teenager.

He married when he was 21 and worked off and on as an auto mechanic. Although his wife was aware of some unusual behavior such as bed-wetting, nightmares, and sleepwalking, she did not find him frightening or exceptionally strange until May 1970, five months before the killings, when he was in a minor auto accident. He was not injured, but he told his wife that immediately after the accident he heard God's voice saying, "If you drive again you will be killed." Frazier's fascination with cars conflicted with his concern about pollution—a conflict which undoubtedly enhanced the significance of an otherwise minor auto accident. Although this episode seemed to "trigger" his psychosis, he was already on the verge of acute paranoid schizophrenia.

From this point on he became rapidly more bizarre and unpredictable. He began to devote himself to implementing God's special mission for him—to save the world from the materialism that was "polluting and destroying the Earth." He incorporated elements of occult philosophy, astrology, phrenology, and numerology into a confusing system of delusional beliefs which were reinforced by direct messages he received from God. He became convinced that the last book of the Bible, Revelation to John, was specifically addressed to him, John Frazier. He talked of his reincarnation and said that he had been born in India ten generations ago and was sent back to the earth to save it from destruction. Early that summer he unsuccessfully tried to recruit 12 disciples (one for each sign of the Zodiac) to renounce all material possessions and go out into the woods with him to live in union with nature. He then began to speak of an impending revolution and wrote in his diary, "The present condition of this world is so that man cannot sustain life as intended by God so I John Frazier believe He will intervein according to the last book or chapter [presumably, Revelation]."

At first those around him thought these strange ideas and pronouncements might be related to a bad drug trip and were only temporary. But as the bizarre and frightening behavior intensified, those who knew him realized this was something beyond the side effects of any drugs Frazier might have consumed. Most of his acquaintances had used drugs such as LSD and amphetamines ("speed") more frequently than Frazier had. Although there is some evidence indicating that excessive use of these drugs may precipitate an acute breakdown in a "latent" or "borderline" schizophrenic, drugs do not *cause* paranoid schizophrenia. They can be aggravating factors, however, just as excessive sugar intake can aggravate a diabetic condition. (In Frazier's case, there was no evidence that he had consumed any drugs in sufficient quantities to cause irreversible brain damage, yet he was acutely psychotic months later in jail where he had no access to drugs of any sort.)

Frazier's wife and mother tried desperately to obtain psychiatric treatment for him, but he had become so paranoid that he saw their efforts as part of a conspiracy: people were plotting against him to prevent him from carrying out his divine mission. He refused psychiatric treatment. On the Fourth of July he left his wife and moved to the area surrounding his mother's house trailer, adjacent to the Ohta property. At times he slept in the cow shed (after constructing a crude drawbridge across the gulch so that he could deny access to his "tormentors"). He would disappear in the woods for days and on various occasions people saw him perched atop an old water tower with a gun, scanning the horizon for hours for the imaginary "them" plotting to destroy him.

The weekend before the killings he visited his wife for the last time. He was unusually agitated and paranoid. He paced back and forth, constantly looking out the windows. He believed that the revolution was at hand, and he said that "some materialists might have to die in the process."

On Monday, October 19, John Frazier carried out his "divine mission." Frazier did not know any of the victims, but in his deranged mind, the occupants of the house had to be sacrificed and the hilltop restored to its natural state. After killing five people he set fires throughout the house. Acquaintances of Frazier, familiar with his delusional ramblings, reported their suspicions to the police. John had gone off into the woods again, but four days after the killings, police found him asleep in the cow shed and arrested him.

Frazier was subsequently tried and convicted on five counts of first-degree murder, and the jury found him to be legally sane. He is currently serving a life sentence in San Quentin. Whether Frazier was evil or mad was the point of contention in his trial—the prosecution contending the former and the defense the latter. Legal insanity aside, after extensive psychiatric examination, there was no doubt in my mind that Frazier suffered from the most serious and most common psychosis—schizophrenia.

Schizophrenics commonly incorporate current controversial topics into their delusions; ecology and revolution were hot topics in 1970. But Frazier's connection with the movements ends there. In fact, his ecology-minded, counterculture friends withdrew from him in fear and bewilderment as he became increasingly psychotic. To a psychiatrist, his symptoms are very familiar. Patients exhibiting the same disordered thinking can be found in almost any psychiatric ward, and descriptions of such patients can be found throughout medical literature in writings as far back as 1400 B.C.

The causes of the various forms of schizophrenia are not known, but are probably multiple—genetic, metabolic, and psychological. As with many disorders of unknown cause (such as cancer) there are nevertheless effective treatments available which can avert an otherwise tragic outcome. Had John Frazier's wife or mother succeeded in their efforts to obtain treatment for him, he might today be one of thousands of similar patients who lead reasonably normal lives with the aid of psychotherapy and anti-psychotic medications which are available and in many cases effective. Many of these patients have had bizarre delusions and violent impulses not unlike Frazier's, but were lucky enough to get into an ongoing treatment program before they began to act out their delusions. I say "lucky" because the likelihood of a given person obtaining appropriate long-term treatment in our chaotic mental health care system often depends upon chance factors. The case history of Edmund Kemper, which now follows, as well as the case history of Herbert Mullin, in Chapter 6, demonstrate additional flaws in the present mental health and "correctional" systems that lead to senseless tragedies.

Sexual Sadism

Unlike the schizophrenic mass murderer, the sadistic murderer does not display bizarre psychotic symptoms and usually has no history of identified mental illness or psychiatric treatment. He is more likely to give thought to avoiding detection by the police and may, in fact, take particular pleasure in his cleverness in this regard. The schizophrenic is much more out of touch with reality and gives little, if any, thought to the possibilities of being arrested. Of all the types of murderers, the sadistic sex murderer is the most likely to repeat his crime.

In rare individuals, for reasons that are not well understood, sexual and violent aggressive impulses merge early in the child's development, ultimately finding expression in violent sexual assaults, and in the most extreme cases, sadistic murders or sex murders. The sadistic murderer derives sexual pleasure from the killing and mutilation or abuse of his victim. Such murderers are almost always male and are usually younger than 35. They usually have few normal social and sexual relationships. In fact, they often have had no experience of normal sexual intercourse. In lieu of normal interpersonal relationships, these individuals have incredibly active fantasy lives. From early childhood on, they engage in extensive daydreaming in which they imagine sadistic scenes and derive great pleasure from this activity. As they get older, they experience additional pleasurable reinforcement by masturbating while imagining brutal acts of killing. Normally there is an intense but ambivalent relationship with the mother. Her death is often one of those fantasized during adolescence. Later on, she may become one of the victims. A Freudian explanation would involve the notion of the Oedipus complex. The killer is in love with the mother and therefore unable to have sex with any other woman. Only by killing the mother can he find release.

The earliest acting out of sadistic impulses often occurs in the early teens in the form of torturing and killing animals such as cats and dogs. An early interest in guns, knives, and various instruments of torture and death is apparent in fantasies, the choice of reading material, and sometimes in drawings. As an adult, a collection of such instruments, proficiency in their use, and an emotional attraction to weapons may be seen which goes far beyond that of any ordinary collector. The method of killing may involve these weapons, but strangulation is sometimes a preferred method. The act of killing itself produces very powerful sexual arousal in these individuals, some of whom will attempt sexual intercourse with the victim.

Case Study: A Sexual Sadist, Edmund Kemper

Edmund Emil Kemper III was the second of three children and the only son born to Edmund and Clarnell Kemper. He bitterly recalls that his father was not around much when he was young and that his parents separated completely when he was 7, after which his mother moved the family from California to Montana. As a result of the move, Ed almost never saw his father. This greatly embittered him, and he blamed his mother entirely. As a child Kemper was physically and socially awkward, always the largest boy in his class. He ultimately grew to 6 feet 9 inches and weighed 280 pounds. He was a loner who dwelled in the world of science fiction and the occult for escape. His mother once wrote, "I was deeply worried during the years about the lack of a father relationship, and so I tried everything I could to compensate for that." According to Ed, this meant she felt a need to punish and ridicule him in order to "make him a man."

His younger sister recalled several events from childhood which seemed only odd to her at the time, but in retrospect seemed "spooky." They were, in fact, early signs of serious psychological disturbance. Ed was fascinated with execution; he would stage his own execution in the form of a childhood "game" in which he had her lead him to a chair, blindfold him, and pull an imaginary lever, after which he would writhe about as if dying in a gas chamber. One Christmas she received a doll from her grandparents, and when she went to play with it later found the head and hands had been cut off. She blamed Ed for this, but he denied it. Another time, she recalled teasing him about a second grade teacher whom she suspected he admired. She taunted him by saying, "Why don't you go and kiss her," and was puzzled at his reply: "If I kiss her I would have to kill her first."

Others also recalled his fascination with guns and knives. Ed described himself as "a weapons freak" and recounted to me recurring fantasies of killing women, his mother in particular. Many times over the years he had, in fact, entered her bedroom at night carrying a weapon and had contemplated killing her.

His first actual killings, however, were of animals. He tortured and killed cats. When Ed was 13, the family cat disappeared; his mother found it in the garbage can—decapitated and cut into pieces. When confronted with accusations of such behavior by his mother or others, Ed would usually deny the charges and blame someone else. For many years, his alibis were so convincing that he succeeded in fooling his mother and teachers. (Unlike the schizophrenic, the sexual sadist makes a serious effort to appear normal to others. Years later, Kemper succeeded in fooling the police so well that they didn't believe his confession until he provided "proof" in the form of bodies.)

In addition to his fantasies of killing his mother, Ed also imagined such things as killing everyone in town and having sexual relations with corpses. As a boy of 9, 10, or 11 he would sneak out of the house at night and from a distance stare at women walking down the street, fantasizing about his desire to love and be loved by them. Even at this early age, however, he felt that relationships with women would be impossible for him. The only kind of activity with women that he could fantasize, with any hope of success, was killing them.

Years later he explained that he "felt very inadequate sexually and sensually and socially," continuing, "so I started out having fantasies about making mad and passionate love to people. . . . But that became dissatisfying because part of me knew that I couldn't really carry these things out. I couldn't follow through with the male end of the responsibility so my fantasies became . . . if I killed them, you know, they couldn't reject me as a man. It was more or less making a doll out of a human being . . . and carrying out my fantasies with a doll, a living human doll."

Ed ran away from home when 13, hoping to go live with his father. But his father made it clear that Ed was not welcome and returned him to his mother. Since she was now finding Ed very difficult to handle and was also planning to remarry, she sent him, protesting and against his will, to live with his paternal grandparents on an isolated ranch in California. For his mother, this was a subtle way of "punishing" both Ed and his father. Ed soon transferred his fantasies about his mother to his domineering grandmother. In less than a year, when he was 15, he killed his grandmother, first shooting and then stabbing her repeatedly. Ed's grandfather was away at the time. Upon his return, Ed shot and killed him before he had a chance to enter the house and discover what had happened to his wife. Ed then telephoned his mother, told her what he had done, sat down, and waited for the police to arrive. In his way, he had avenged the rejection of both his mother and father.

Since he was a minor, Kemper was turned over to the California Youth Authority. Because of the serious and unusual nature of the offense, it was assumed that Kemper was "inappropriate" for any of the CYA facilities. Consequently, he spent 4 of the next 5 years in a maximum security mental hospital, where he received minimal treatment. In 1969, when he was 21, he was transferred back to the Youth Authority. The parole board subsequently discharged Ed to his mother, a disastrous situation from Kemper's point of view. (There were no psychiatrists or psychologists on the parole board, and in this particular case no consideration was given to psychiatric reports about Ed's feelings toward his mother.) Upon his release, he received no psychological or psychiatric treatment.

Repeated arguments with his mother again erupted, reviving his old fantasies about killing her. Substitute victims before had been dolls, cats, and finally his grandparents. Now his victims would be college girls. (His mother had moved to Santa Cruz, California, and was on the administrative staff of the University of California at Santa Cruz. A reserved parking sticker which she obtained for Ed's car gave him easy access to UCSC coeds.)

Between May 7, 1972, and April 21, 1973, Kemper killed eight women by shooting, stabbing, and strangulation. He acted out his childhood fantasies by cutting off limbs of the victims, attempting sexual relations with the corpses, and committing acts of cannibalism. The first six victims were young female hitchhikers. Despite his past record, police never suspected Kemper. In fact, Kemper associated regularly with the local police at a Santa Cruz bar. On April 21, 1973, the day before Easter, Kemper killed his mother and one of her friends. After decapitation, he cut out his mother's larynx and put it down the garbage disposal. "This seemed appropriate," he said, "as much as she'd bitched and screamed and yelled at me over the years."

He left an anonymous note in her apartment to taunt the police and drove off, fantasizing a nationwide manhunt for the "coed killer." He drove nonstop as far as Pueblo, Colorado, listening all the while for an "all-points bulletin" on the radio. After three days passed without any radio bulletins or newspaper headlines, Kemper called the Santa Cruz police to turn himself in. They told him to call back. He did, again and again, each time giving more details about the killings in an effort to impress them. Finally, he convinced them to have him arrested. When the police picked him up, he was waiting in a public phone booth.

Kemper was tried, convicted, and sentenced to life imprisonment. He was found legally sane, as was Frazier. Although Ed had spent several years in custody in a mental hospital, it had not helped him. There may be a point in the sexual sadist's development beyond which sexual and violent aggressive impulses are inextricably interwoven. If such persons are to be treated effectively, treatment would probably need to begin in childhood, early in the development of the sadistic impulses. It is rare, however, that such persons can be (or are) identified this early. This being the case, should sexual sadists, once identified, be locked up for life or executed? What if they are identified but have not yet committed a crime? I will return to these questions in a later chapter.

Sex Murders of Other Times and Other Places

The only significant difference between Kemper and other sex killers throughout history was his ability to find his victims easily near freeway on-ramps. From 1962 to 1964 the "Boston Strangler" kept a city in terror with a series of 13 sex murders. Some of the victims were young, single women, but most of them were older women ranging in age from 55 to 85. The strangler gained entry simply by knocking on apartment doors and explaining that the building manager had hired him to check and repair leaks in the plumbing. Some of the women were suspicious enough to query through a bolted door, "How do I know you're not the Boston Strangler?" His disarming matter-of-fact reply would be, "Well, if you don't want the repair work done, that's all right—I'll leave." This tactic usually resulted in the women opening the door and sometimes apologizing that a woman living alone "has to be careful these days." Nodding knowingly, he would proceed to the bathroom and ask the unwitting victim to "come in here and take a look at this." When cornered in the bathroom, the victim was suddenly confronted with a killer rather than a plumber. He would warn the victim to be quiet or she would get hurt and then would tie her up with nylon stockings, scarves, and other items he would find around the apartment. Once immobilized and blindfolded or gagged, death usually came quickly by strangulation. Subsequent attempts at sexual relations were usually unsuccessful; sometimes the strangler would have a spontaneous orgasm (as did Kemper) while killing. There was also evidence to indicate he had taken photographs of at least one victim (as had Kemper). To taunt police, he left a greeting card on the foot of his last victim, murdered January 4, 1964, reading "Happy New Year."

Because of legal technicalities relating to the admissibility of his confessions and a myriad of other factors, the "Boston Strangler," Albert De Salvo, at the age of 33 was arrested and subsequently convicted only of armed robbery. He was sentenced to life imprisonment without standing trial for the sex murders, and is still serving his sentence.

Eighteen years earlier the police of the city of Chicago undertook what was called the "largest manhunt in history." In January of 1946, a 6-year-old first-grader named Suzanne Degnan had been kidnapped from her bedroom while asleep. Her dismembered body was later found in various neighborhood sewers. For six months the crime went unsolved. Seven months earlier, in June 1945, a 43-year-old widow had been fatally stabbed and slashed in her apartment. Although her body was nude when found, she had not been raped. That December a 33-year-old unmarried secretary was stabbed and shot to death in her apartment. Again, pathologists' reports indicated that rape had not occurred, despite the fact that the victim's pajama bottoms had been removed and her pajama top was wrapped loosely about her neck. A startling message was written across the bedroom wall with lipstick:

For heavens
Sake catch me
Before I kill more
I cannot control myself

"The Lipstick Murderer," as he was called, was not identified until June 26, 1946, when a 17-year-old named William George Heirens was arrested for robbery. He was a student at the University of Chicago, and in his dormitory room police found two suitcases filled with pistols, surgical equipment, jewelry, watches, and war bonds. There were pictures of Hitler, Goering, Goebbels, and other Nazis in the room. Heirens' fingerprints were routinely checked against fingerprints found on a note left at the Degnan home (7,000 fingerprints of other arrested persons had already been checked). Heirens' prints matched and he ultimately confessed to the three sex murders, as well as to some 300 burglaries since age 12. The burglaries ("breaking and entering") were sexually motivated. While entering a window Heirens experienced an erection and sometimes an orgasm, something he did not experience by any other means. He usually stole women's underwear along with objects of greater value, if present. (He actually began stealing women's underwear from neighborhood clotheslines at age 9 and progressed to burglary 3 years later.)

A psychiatric examination following his arrest included these observations:

> He was a solitary child and youth, sensitive but difficult to know. Apparently no one ever had a close or confidential relationship with him. . . . In the 7th and 8th grades excessive daydreaming was reported. . . . It was clear that normal sex stimulation and experience were unpleasant, indeed "repulsive," to him, and . . . created in him a negative emotional state. He found them improper in the conduct of others; he never spoke of them except in condemnation, as, for example, of the young men in the university who had brought a girl into their rooms at night.

When questioned about his reading habits, he mentioned reading about "masochism, fetishism, sadism, and flagellation." It was further revealed that the sadistic fantasies Heirens had entertained for years far exceeded those he had acted out.

William Heirens was tried and found legally sane. He pleaded guilty to 30 counts of burglary as well as the three murders and one other assault to commit murder. He was sentenced to life imprisonment.

Many aspects of Heirens' personal history and mental state were similar, if not identical, to the general description of sex murderers mentioned earlier. One facet of Heirens' history deserves special mention, namely, the long succession of burglaries. Sex murderers rarely, if ever, have criminal records for lesser sex offenses such as exhibitionism or voyeurism, nor are they homosexuals. However, if they do have a previous criminal record, it is most likely for offenses of breaking and entering. Such persons are known to experience sexual arousal when entering a bedroom window. Fetishism involving women's underwear is also not unique to William Heirens, but this is not as readily suspected and detected as burglary.

Sex murderers are not a product of the times. Other countries and other centuries have produced sex murderers similar to those I have described from recent U.S. history. Peter Kürten of Düsseldorf, Germany, committed at least 13 murders and many more assaults and attempted murders between 1899 and 1930. He finally came under medical observation and confessed his crimes, for which he was executed in 1931. Kürten began torturing and killing animals for pleasure at age nine. When he was 14 he attempted intercourse with a girl, but was unsuccessful. Soon after, however, he strangled a squirrel and experienced the first of many orgasms achieved in conjunction with a sadistic act. For several years his primary sexual outlet involved killing animals, but then he was arrested and imprisoned on a theft charge. During his prison term he perfected the ability to achieve orgasm by fantasizing about sadistic acts, since masturbation and homosexuality (the only other sexual outlets available in prison) were repugnant to him. Following his release, he began a career of killing that included strangling, beating, and stabbing. The wide variation in the number of stab wounds or blows on his victims was readily explained by Kürten: he stabbed or struck his victims as many times as it required for him to achieve orgasm on a given occasion. Like other multiple sex murderers, he viewed his victims as objects for his pleasure rather than fellow human beings. Therefore, he neither felt nor expressed any remorse for his victims or his deeds, although he did express some regret for the victims' families (as did Kemper). Also, typically, he took pride in describing his crimes in great detail.

"Jack the Ripper" was never caught, but taunted the police and the press about his crimes and identity in such a way as to assure great publicity and a place in history (a conscious goal of many such killers). Practically every European country had at least one murderer of the "Ripper" (mutilator) type during the 19th century.

Perhaps the most massive in scope and scale of the sadistic murderers was Gilles de Rais, born in France in 1404, and heir to an immense fortune. By his early twenties, Gilles de Rais had become chief lieutenant and protector of Joan of Arc. He was extremely devoted to her, and following her capture and execution in 1431, he retreated in apparent grief to his castle, where over the next 9 years he tortured and murdered hundreds of children. He was brought to trial in 1440 and sentenced to death.

Other Varieties of Mass Murder

The types of offenders I have just described are the ones commonly associated with the term "mass murderer"; other kinds of multiple killing, for various reasons, are not. One such multiple killing occurs when a despondent spouse, usually the husband, often recently separated or divorced, kills his wife and children and then commits, or at least attempts to commit, suicide. These individuals are subsumed by feelings of anger, jealousy, and depression which may be of psychotic proportions.

One of the most unusual and bizarre multiple murders of modern times was the killing of 44 persons aboard an airplane November 1, 1955, just outside of Denver. Two weeks later John Gilbert Graham confessed to placing a homemade bomb containing 25 sticks of dynamite in the luggage of his mother who was a passenger on the plane. He had long resented his mother, who had rejected him repeatedly as a child. After his father left his mother, when he was 18 months old, he was turned over to his maternal grandmother. His grandmother died when he was 6 and his mother subsequently placed him in an institution for fatherless boys, despite his repeated pleas to come home. His mother had remarried, and he frequently ran away from the institution to be with her. She sent him back on a number of occasions, but finally, when he was 11, she relented and allowed him to live with her and her husband. By then he had already been in trouble for fire-setting and torturing animals.

He had grave doubts about his masculinity, which seemed to be exacerbated by his mother's interfering with his business and by a recent sterilization operation. (His wife had almost died in childbirth, and the operation was the only foolproof contraception available at the time.) After his arrest he said of his mother, "Down deep I think she resented me, little things she would do to aggravate me. . . . She held something over me that I couldn't get [out] from under. When the plane left the ground a load came off my shoulders, I watched her go off for the last time. I felt happier than I ever felt before in my life. . . . I just didn't think about the other people on the plane. . . . I deserve to be taken out and shot."

Following his conviction he adamantly opposed any appeals to higher courts and was executed in the gas chamber of the Colorado State Penitentiary.

One final type of mass killing is known as *collective crime*. This phenomenon involves multiple killers, as well as multiple victims. Group psychology, as well as individual psychology, is involved. Several examples from recent history are well known and will therefore be mentioned just briefly here.

Charles Manson and five of his 60-member "family" killed actress Sharon Tate and four others in her Los Angeles home in August 1969. Others were killed during the four months which elapsed before Manson and his five followers were arrested. One of the five, 21-year-old Linda Kasabian, was granted immunity from prosecution in exchange for her testimony. Charles "Tex" Watson, charged with 6 murders, was found mentally incompetent and was committed to Atascadero State Hospital. Manson and the other three (women) were convicted, and are now serving life prison terms; they refused psychiatric examinations and are therefore presumed to be sane under the law.

Mass killings committed by military personnel during wartime are referred to as massacres. The best-known instance from the war in Vietnam occurred in 1968 at My Lai; as many as 500 South Vietnamese were killed by American soldiers led by U.S. Army Lt. William Calley.

The most horrifying collective crime of this century was the systematic extermination of some six million European Jews by the Nazis during World War II. The details of this crime of genocide are both well known and well documented, and hopefully will never be forgotten. Despite a common myth to the contrary, the planners, organizers, and executioners of the S.S. "final solution" were not insane by psychiatric standards, so far as we know. Terrorist mass killings, such as occurred at the 1972 Olympic Games in Munich, when 11 Israeli athletes were killed by Arab guerrillas, have political as well as genocidal overtones.

At least one characteristic of collective crimes resembles a phenomenon seen in sexual sadist murderers—that is, the dehumanization of the victims, or perception of them as objects. To the sex murderer the victims may be viewed as "life-size dolls" rather than fellow human beings. In collective crimes, the victims may be perceived as "enemies of the state" or "enemies of the revolution" or some other kind of faceless, inhuman *objects*. This perspective greatly facilitates the act of killing, since it prevents the killer from identifying with the victims as mothers, fathers, children, people who love and are loved, people whose lives have meaning.

Courtroom sketch of Herbert Mullin, by Don Juhlin.

CHAPTER SIX

"MURDER PREVENTS EARTHQUAKES": A CASE STUDY OF HERBERT MULLIN

BETWEEN 1970 AND 1973, Santa Cruz, California, came to be described by its district attorney, Peter Chang, as "the murder capital of the world." This characterization resulted primarily from the fact that three Santa Cruz men, John Frazier, Edmund Kemper, and Herbert Mullin, killed a total of 26 persons during this period. Judge Charles Franich, prosecutor Chang, public defender James Jackson, investigator Harold Cartwright, psychologist David Marlowe, and I had thought the Frazier trial would be an isolated episode that brought us in contact with each other for a brief period. Instead, we found ourselves involved almost continuously over a 3-year period in an unprecedented sequence of mass murder, investigations, and trials. Although the Frazier and Kemper cases attracted the most publicity, the Mullin case was the most classic example of a mentally ill mass murderer. It was the only case of the three in which all experts for the defense and prosecution agreed on the diagnosis—paranoid schizophrenia. The story of Herbert Mullin demonstrates the salient features of this disorder as well as some tragic shortcomings of our present system of mental health care.

The Context of a Delusion

The San Andreas fault runs south from San Francisco just inland from the Pacific Coast. The fault acts up periodically, causing minor tremors and, occasionally, major earthquakes such as the great San Francisco earthquake of 1906. During the fall of 1972, San Francisco newspapers reported the predictions of a self-styled expert who, having predicted the 1971 earthquake in the Los Angeles area, now determined that a major earthquake along the San Andreas fault would occur on January 4, 1973, and would exceed in magnitude the great San Francisco earthquake. January 4, 1973, is now long past, and the much-publicized earthquake never occurred.

Herbert William Mullin had a theory all his own about earthquakes: "We human beings, through the history of the world, have protected our continents from cataclysmic earthquakes by murder." He continued, "In other words, a minor natural disaster avoids a major natural disaster." How did Mullin figure this? If one took the earthquake records of China, which were the oldest, he explained, and then studied all the demographic data of births and deaths, "you could come out with a percentage of people that have been steadily dying violently in order to prove to the great Creator, who created the earth and put it in orbit around the sun, just to prove to Him that we are willing to die . . . if He can keep . . . the earth in orbit and keep the continents intact so that there isn't any cataclysmic earthquakes or violent tidal waves or anything." He concluded, "We human beings . . . have found murder decreases the number of natural disasters and the extent of the devastation of these disasters; therefore, we will always murder."

Between October 13, 1972, and February 13, 1973, Herbert Mullin killed 13 people. He killed to avert the great earthquake and therefore save thousands of lives. In Mullin's mind, the connection was simple. He recounted during his trial that anyone who studied the Bible, as he did in school, could understand it:

> You read in the Bible about Jonah . . . . Jonah stood up and said, ". . . If somebody doesn't die, you know, all 13 of us are going to die." And he jumped overboard . . . and he was drowned. . . . And the sea . . . in about a half hour or so it calmed down. . . . And so they get to town and they go to a bar and they tell the people at the bar about Jonah, and they say, "We think Jonah saved our life by committing suicide," and the people at the bar say, "Well, maybe that will help us," so they go out and kill somebody. So the story goes.

Childhood

He was a normal boy.—Jean Mullin

God, I loved the kid.—Martin Mullin

Martin and Jean Mullin had their first child, a daughter, shortly after the Japanese bombed Pearl Harbor. Jean was still in the hospital when Martin told her he was going to volunteer for the Army. By the end of World War II, Martin Mullin had worked his way up to the position of company commander in an automatic weapons battalion. It was the high point of his life in terms of status and personal achievement.

On April 18, 1947, with the war over and Martin back in civilian life, Jean Mullin gave birth to a son, Herbert, in Salinas, California, just south of Santa Cruz. Twenty-five years later Herb attached great significance to his birthdate—and the fact that the San Francisco earthquake of 1906 also occurred on April 18. He also claimed that the death of Albert Einstein on April 18, 1955, had somehow prevented him from being killed in Vietnam, but I was never quite able to follow this line of thought. Testifying at his trial in 1973, Herb rambled about "the birth position placement director" who has the power "to put people's entities in bodies that would be in a combat zone, and then those bodies would be killed." Apparently, Herb believed his father had made such a petition to the "placement director," but that it was negated by Albert Einstein's sacrificial death on Herb's behalf.

Martin Mullin worked in a small furniture store in Salinas after his discharge from the Army, until 1948 when he moved the family to Walnut Creek, east of San Francisco, and took a job with a larger furniture store in nearby Oakland. Jean Mullin was a devout Catholic, and by 1948 she was taking Herb's 6-year-old sister to Mass with her. Her husband, baptized a Lutheran, later attended the Methodist church. After leaving Salinas, he started attending Mass with the family and in 1950 converted to Catholicism. Jean and Martin agreed that the children would receive instruction in the Catholic church.

In 1952, another move took the Mullin family to San Francisco, which remained their home for 11 years. Herb attended kindergarten at a public school, but the following year his parents enrolled him at St. Stephen's School. He attended parochial schools through his sophomore year in high school.

Martin Mullin's hours as a furniture salesman were long, and the pay provided few luxuries. Martin was frequently on the road, but tried to compensate by involving himself with Herb's activities whenever he could. "I even got mixed up with the Boy Scouts when he became a Scout. . . . When he was about 8 we got the troop mixed up in the West of Twin Peaks Baseball League, and I wound up as a coach in that darn thing for 4 years—fighting all the mothers and fathers who thought they had All-Americans as sons. I did it for Herb—God, I loved the kid, I loved the kid very, very dearly."

Their neighborhood seemed a good one for a growing, physically active boy. A lake and an undeveloped park area were nearby. Martin recalled to me that "Herb and other boys dug trenches, built treehouses there, and stuff like that." Herb's mother felt he enjoyed elementary school at St. Stephen's and that he got along well there. He received good grades and was rarely in trouble. "He was normal," she recounted. "I had to go to school a couple of times when he was in grammar school—Sister Mary Annette called us in once when Herb carved something in some newly painted benches, but he was very alert, very agreeable." Martin was going to spank Herb for the bench-carving incident, but he told Sister Mary Annette that he had recently given him a good spanking for a "curfew violation," and she interrupted him and said, "No, please don't beat him."

Grammar School

I never had one single person come from any grammar school for dinner. At age 6 or 8 that experience of receiving communion and going to confession tends to make a person extremely gullible.—Herbert W. Mullin, during his trial

Herb told me in his jail cell that he remembered living in Walnut Creek as a young boy and seeing his sister go off to school on a bus in the morning. He had looked forward to reaching the age when he could walk to the bus stop with her and take the same bus to school. Then they moved. According to Herb, his parents thought, "Well, if we move to San Francisco . . . that way he won't get to ride the bus and we'll offer up that agony, you know, that he'll go through psychologically . . . we'll offer that up to accomplish our prayers for the family. So we go to San Francisco and I don't have the same friends that I used to have; everything is just cut off."

It is unlikely that Herb actually experienced these feelings of persecution at the time, but in retrospect he was genuinely convinced that events after 1952 represented deliberate sadistic efforts of his parents and others to "retard" his development. He told me, in the course of psychiatric consultation just prior to his trial, "I believe my parents consciously intended to retard my social and sexual awareness. They are killjoy reincarnationists. They believe that by spoiling the enjoyment of others they improve their birth-position in the very next life."

Testifying at the trial, Herb said, "Other persons my age would think, 'Should I ask Herb to go riding on a bicycle to the park?' . . . And they said, 'No, I don't think I will ask Herb, because if I help him to enjoy life a little bit, his father is going to have me killed in my next life, and

I don't want that, so I won't even phone him up.' "

When Santa Cruz Public Defender James Jackson asked: "How did your father get this word out to the other kids?" Herb answered: "Telepathically, I imagine. On some occasions he even probably went door to door asking them, you know, to refrain from teaching me the facts of life. . . . I never had one single person from any grammar school for dinner. . . . Normal children by then have learned Jonah's philosophy that one person committing suicide or getting in an automobile accident or jumping off of a bridge, or any of the various other ways of exterminating life from the body—that keeps the coastal areas from experiencing earthquakes, either small or large, to some extent."

Before the trial, while trying to sort out his thoughts in his maximum security cell in the San Mateo County Jail, Herb wrote:

> When I was in the second grade they told me that Jesus Christ, the person, actually lives in the Holy Eucharist. I chose to believe them then; I choose not to believe them now. It is a lie, designed to induce naïvete and gullibility in young children. Thereby making them suseseptible to receive and carry out telepathic subconscious suicide orders. . . . One day I took a knife and cut a wood bench. . . . I felt ignored and frustrated. . . . My parents and teachers tried to retard me. . . . I feel as if their is a conspiracy against me. I've told my parents this and they say I'm crazy and imagining it. I don't know what to do about this situation. Mental cruelty is certainly present. Can I sue my parents? Actually I feel like killing the people responsible. They think by practicing killjoyism on me they will trade consciousness with me in the next universal life time.

High School and College

Riorden High School was a Catholic school and he did resent the attitude of the brothers, so he was quite happy when we decided to move down to Santa Cruz when he went into his junior year.—Jean Mullin

There's one turning point here that we're probably missing, and that was the summer of 1965 when he lost his very best boyfriend.—Martin Mullin

In the summer of 1963, the Mullin family moved again. Herb by then had completed his freshman and sophomore years at a Catholic high school in San Francisco, which he disliked even more than St. Stephen's, where he had completed the first eight grades. Martin Mullin was then 54 and disenchanted with the life of a traveling furniture salesman. The

Mullins had relatives near Santa Cruz, and they decided to move there.

Herb's sister stayed in San Francisco, where she was attending San Francisco State College, and in 1965 she married and moved north with her husband to Sebastopol to raise a family and grow Christmas trees for a living. (Unlike Ed Kemper's sister, Herb Mullin's sister had no basis for thinking her brother was a potential mass murderer. Furthermore, she had no basis for even supposing Herb might become seriously mentally ill someday—much less that his first psychotic breakdown would occur at their home.)

Martin Mullin got a civil service job with the post office. Herb was a fairly good student and athlete at San Lorenzo Valley High School. For the first time in his life, he had both a steady girlfriend, Loretta, and a close boyfriend, Dean. Dean and Herb both belonged to an informal group of high school athletes calling themselves the "Zeros." For a change, Herb was a part of a group he liked.

Herb's happiest year was probably 1964. For the first time he had an active social life with people his own age. Herb and Dean went to the beach together, played games, and doubledated. In June 1965, Herb graduated 43rd in his high school class of 134. Within a matter of weeks, his friend Dean was killed in an automobile accident. Of all the "Zeros," Herb was the most upset. He insisted on participating in the funeral arrangements with Dean's mother. After the funeral he would sit alone in his room for hours at a time. A friend later remarked that the way Herb had arranged various objects around Dean's picture in his room "kind of resembled a shrine." Herb's strange behavior at this time was the first indication of mental illness. However, the onset of schizophrenia is often insidious, and since Herb had never before given his parents any reason for concern, they were inclined to view this period as "something he would get over." They had no way of knowing that the serious symptoms of paranoid schizophrenia rarely appear before the twenties, although early indications may appear in the late teens.

By September Herb had pulled himself together enough to attend a nearby junior college. One day the following March, while at the beach in Santa Cruz, Herb ran into Jim Gianera, a casual acquaintance from San Lorenzo Valley High School. Jim was smoking marijuana and offered Herb a joint. With some reluctance Herb tried it. Jim also told Herb he opposed the war and mentioned that becoming a conscientious objector was one way of avoiding the draft. It was one of a million such encounters in those days. Many college students were experimenting with marijuana and many were talking about the war. Jim was getting heavily involved in drug usage and sales. Herb was not a close associate of Jim Gianera. In fact, Herb was still living at home, and his parents never heard him mention Jim's name, although Martin thought he might have seen Gianera with Herb once in high school.

From Student to Patient

Marijuana induces dementia praecox, you know. . . . If Gianera had given me some Benzedrine instead, I would have become an artist.—Herbert W. Mullin, during an interview in his cell

Herb completed a 2-year program in civil highway technology at Cabrillo College in June 1967, but during the last year there his interests had shifted significantly. In September of 1966, Herb had talked of joining the Army Corps of Engineers upon graduating from Cabrillo. In September of 1967, Herb enrolled at San Jose State College with vague plans of studying Eastern religions. He stayed at San Jose less than three months, but during that period he decided to become a conscientious objector rather than join the Army or be drafted. In addition to marijuana, he was now experimenting with LSD, but his usage was minor compared to that of many of his peers.

His romance with Loretta had been on and off since high school, but early in 1967 she agreed to marry him, and he bought an engagement ring. By that fall she began to have serious doubts, which were reinforced by her parents. She was concerned about Herb's "weird behavior," his violent outbursts, and his recent comments that he thought he might be a homosexual. Her mother was frightened by his recent moody, unpredictable behavior—totally unlike his behavior in high school when he was known as a good student and athlete, and was voted "most likely to succeed." Loretta's father, a former military man, was most put off by Herb's new stance toward the Army. He called Herb a coward to his face. Loretta broke the engagement early in 1968. Herb was upset, but not as upset as he had been over Dean's death. In addition, he was now preoccupied with applying for conscientious objector status. Herb was granted C.O. status and went to work for Goodwill Industries. He worked for Goodwill first in Santa Cruz and later managed their San Luis Obispo store. In February 1969, however, he came home and announced that he was going to India to study religion. Herb's ideas were becoming more and more unrealistic, his parents thought. They finally convinced him to move north to Sebastopol, where his sister and her husband had agreed to give Herb a job on their Christmas tree farm.

One month later, Martin and Jean Mullin came to Sebastopol for a family dinner in honor of their 29th wedding anniversary. At the dinner table Herb showed symptoms that were unmistakably bizarre, frightening—and unlike anything the family had ever seen before. Whenever Herb's brother-in-law, Al, picked up his fork or spoke, Herb would also pick up his fork or would repeat exactly what Al had just said. This persisted throughout dinner. "I just remember it was such a shocking thing—that he wasn't himself. He was like a vegetable, imitating everything Al did," his mother said.

A standard psychiatric textbook includes this observation on some of the symptoms of schizophrenia: "The patient may show an automatic obedience to verbal directions without reference to their appropriateness or significance. Instead of answering a question, he may repeat it in a parrotlike manner—*echolalia*. He may also imitate the movement of a person in his immediate environment—*echopraxia*."

It took the family almost 24 hours to convince Herb to voluntarily admit himself to the nearest mental hospital in Mendocino. Herb was admitted to Mendocino State Hospital March 30, 1969, with a diagnosis of "schizophrenic reaction, manifested by distortions of associations and affect, hallucinations, echolalia, echopraxia, and general deterioration." Herb was hospitalized until May 9, 1969. During these six weeks, he was generally uncooperative with the staff and with the treatment program. Although after a while he began to talk to some of the other patients, he spoke primarily of yoga and his personalized version of Oriental philosophy. At the time of his discharge, it was noted that his "prognosis is poor. It seems that all recommendations, programming, and so forth, have fallen on 'deaf ears.' " As a voluntary patient, he could not be forced to accept treatment or to remain in the hospital, and Herb wanted to leave.

Herb drifted to South Lake Tahoe for a few months, where he worked briefly as a dishwasher. He quit his job on August 30, 1969. A few days later, ranger Ron Lang was patrolling an isolated area of a state park near Santa Cruz and came across a young man seated beneath a lean-to with his legs crossed and his hands in his lap, staring straight ahead. The lean-to was constructed of saplings which appeared to have been cut nearby, in violation of park regulations. The young man remained mute despite repeated questions by Lang. He appeared to be in a trance, but was finally evicted from the park with the assistance of some other rangers. Herb returned to Santa Cruz.

He managed to hold a job at a gas station for a brief period, but then he moved south to San Luis Obispo. He stayed briefly with a friend, John, whom he had known casually, but Herb's behavior was too bizarre and frightening to be tolerated for long. Herb spoke of "hearing voices" and "receiving messages"; he had experienced hallucinations before, but now they were different. Instead of saying things about Herb, the voices were now telling Herb to *do* certain things (*command hallucinations* in psychiatric jargon). Furthermore, Herb was obeying the voices: they told him to shave his head and he did so; they told him to burn his penis, and he did so with a lighted cigarette. Then he began to make bizarre, forceful, homosexual advances toward John. He made a remark to the effect that "murder is an act of love." On October 31, 1969, Halloween, Herb was committed to the psychiatric ward of the San Luis Obispo County Hospital, on the basis that "as a result of mental disorder, said person is a danger to others, a danger to himself, and gravely disabled."

During this hospitalization, Herb wrote letters voluminously—to his doctors, to his parents, to politicians and other public figures who had never heard of Herbert Mullin. The letters included his thoughts on religion and the state of the universe. He often concluded his letters with the phrase: "Respectfully yours, a human sacrifice, Herb Mullin."

Although Herb was treated with anti-psychotic drugs which are usually effective in alleviating the acute symptoms of paranoid schizophrenia, such as hallucinations and delusions, he showed only slight improvement. His thinking was described as "paralogical, bizarre, and grandiose." For a while, he carried a Bible with him constantly, exhorting the other patients on the ward to follow him in "changing the spiritual nature of the world." After a few weeks, Herb began pressuring his doctor and his father to allow him to return to Santa Cruz. They reluctantly agreed, on the condition that Herb would continue to receive treatment at the Santa Cruz Community Mental Health Outpatient Clinic. On November 23, 1969, he was discharged. The final diagnosis again was "schizophrenic reaction." The prognosis was characterized as "grave."

Records from the Santa Cruz Health Clinic indicate that "Herbert Mullin, a 22-year-old single man, short, stocky, and even-featured, first appeared in the clinic on November 24, 1969." In the subsequent months anti-psychotic medications were again prescribed for Herb, but he did not take them regularly. He was assigned to a therapy group, which he attended sporadically because the group meetings conflicted at times with his work schedule. (He now had a job as a busboy at a nearby hotel.) A social worker at the clinic noted, "Around May of 1970 Herb began to branch out a bit and make a concerted effort at being more actively involved in life. This included dating, attendance at various peace organizations, and once again taking up his pursuit of religious perfection within the yoga discipline. I was never clear as to whether this constituted some sort of deterioration or progress."

On June 25, 1970, Herb Mullin took off for Hawaii against his parents' advice. Shortly after his arrival in Hawaii, Herb was again in a mental hospital. He seemed to recognize that he needed help and voluntarily applied for admission to the Maui Mental Health Service. A psychologist who examined him noted that "his personality profile indicates strong aggressive impulses which are tenuously controlled by denial and a passive stance. He has lately had insomnia and fearful fantasies. Diagnosis: Schizophrenia." This diagnosis was made independent of any knowledge of his California hospitalizations. (There is no simple mechanism for obtaining previous hospital records. Prior to Mullin's trial, it took us months to assemble all of his records, some of which were seemingly "buried" in remote storage facilities.)

According to hospital records from Hawaii, his stay was marked by several bizarre incidents, such as wandering off the ward to look for work while dressed in a hospital gown (he was returned by the police), and engaging others in illogical ramblings on the subjects of yoga and his desire to spread nonviolence. Again, anti-psychotic medication was prescribed, and he was instructed to take it regularly. Finally, his parents were contacted for money to purchase a plane ticket for his return; a police officer then escorted him to the airport and put him on a plane bound for San Francisco on July 23, 1970.

His parents picked him up at the San Francisco airport, but before they had traveled halfway back to Santa Cruz, they became so frightened by his bizarre behavior that they stopped en route, and Martin Mullin called the Mountain View, California, police to see whether Herb could be admitted to nearby Agnews State Hospital. A police officer listened briefly to the story and said something about lacking jurisdiction and told the Mullins to return to Santa Cruz. Ten days later Herb was arrested by the Santa Cruz police for strange behavior on the street, which was assumed to be the result of "being under the influence of drugs." In fact, he was displaying symptoms which were only partially controlled by the medications he had in his pocket. Records indicate that he was placed in jail, his medications were taken away (standard procedure in many jails), and during the night he became hyperactive and began singing loudly. When brought before the judge the next day, Mullin demanded that he legalize marijuana and LSD. The judge ordered that Herb be sent to Santa Cruz General Hospital for observation, and the criminal charges against him were subsequently dropped. Back on his medications again, Herb became less noisy and belligerent and was discharged from the hospital on August 5, 1970, with a diagnosis of schizophrenia, paranoid type.

Until the following May 31, Herb lived a marginal existence in Santa

Courtroom sketch of Public Defender James Jackson and Herbert Mullin, by Don Juhlin.

Cruz, driving a truck for Goodwill Industries and sporadically attending a local drug abuse clinic. Then, abruptly, he quit his job and moved to San Francisco. For the next year he lived in cheap hotels in the skid-row section of the city. Until September of 1972, Herb remained essentially out of touch with his family and old friends. He spent his time writing, drawing, reading, and boxing at a nearby gym. Then, on September 15, 1972, Herb was evicted from his hotel room in San Francisco and moved back to his parents' home.

One of the first things he did on his return was challenge his father to a boxing match. When Herb was young, he and his father would sometimes spar open-handed in the backyard or in the kitchen while waiting for dinner to be served. But, as his father described it to me,

> Right after he came home from San Francisco, he closed in on me. He hit me a couple of times right smack on the jaw, just boom, boom, boom, and he says, "Come on, let's go, it won't last long," just like that, and that's the last time I sparred with him, believe me. He scared me. It was such a departure from what we had normally done all our lives. . . . He was not the same kid we had raised and known. Periodically, for instance, we'd be talking about something in normal family conversation at the dinner table and Herb would suddenly say, "Do you know how many ants there are in an ant colony?" Clear out in left field, just as though he'd turned to a page in an encyclopedia and is interjecting that thought on top of what the normal conversation had been.

Martin Mullin now made inquiries about long-term hospitalization for Herb. It was obvious that Herb could not be handled at home, and Santa Cruz had no facility for the kind of care he needed. Herb's uncle voiced the same concerns. Something about Herb's manner was alarming. Herb had been telling his uncle about his reincarnation theory, which Herb somehow related to plans he was making for swimming the English Channel.

The Mullins soon discovered that long-term hospitalization was out of the question. Under Governor Ronald Reagan a plan to phase out the state mental hospital system had been devised and implemented, and by June 1972 many of the state hospitals in California had been closed or were in the process of closing down. Although partly motivated by budget-cutting concerns, the plan envisioned community-based mental health facilities that would provide care closer to home for those in need of hospitalization or outpatient treatment. Federal funding had been previously appropriated by Congress for the construction and staffing of such centers, but between 1972 and 1974 these funds were cut back and then eliminated from the federal budget, and most of the projected federally-funded community mental health centers were never built. Many former state mental hospital patients ended up in boarding houses in run-down neighborhoods of San Francisco, San Jose, and Los Angeles (neighborhoods that have come to be known as "psychiatric ghettos"). Some patients were able to live with relatives and a few could afford private hospitals. A private hospital, at $100 per day, was not possible on Martin Mullin's salary.

Meanwhile, Herb's paranoid delusions were becoming more and more grandiose. Herb wrote to the United Nations requesting "demographic data and any information pertaining to how many people die every day, week, month, and year, and their respective ages." He received a reply, referring him to his local public library. He pieced together some of his fragmented thoughts with "telepathic" messages which were now more frequent. The telepathic messages he was receiving seemed to him to be coming from his father. One message could be heard above all the others and carried with it a sense of urgency—"Herb, I want you to kill me somebody."

Auditory hallucinations are characteristic of paranoid schizophrenia (in contrast to the visual hallucinations associated with the use of LSD and other hallucinogenic drugs). The "voices" of the paranoid schizophrenic usually consist of derogatory remarks about the patient or other declarative propositions. Rarely, the "voices" order the patient to perform certain acts and even more rarely, these "orders" involve acts of violence. A patient with a history of acting upon such hallucinatory commands is, without continuous treatment, potentially dangerous.

From Patient to Mass Murderer

Let it be known to the nations of earth and to the people that inhabit it, this document carries more power than any other written before. Such a tragedy as what has happen to us should not have happened and because of this action which I take of my own free will I am making it impossible for it to occur again. For while I can be here I must guide and protect my dynasty.—Herbert W. Mullin, 1972

The voices became louder and more persistent in October of 1972, and they sounded like Martin Mullin. The message was, "Why won't you give me anything? Go kill somebody—move!" Herb was living more and more in a delusional world that he shared with no one. He had long since abandoned his psychiatric treatment and medications, and his parents were finding it impossible to "reason with him."

Herb's writings over the next several months were filled with references to Albert Einstein, charts and prayers relating to reincarnation of the "H.C. Baker Dynasty" (Herb's grandfather), birth rates, death rates, terms from seismology (like "thrust fault," "gravity fault," and "lag fault") and quotations from the Bible, such as Job 14:14, "If a man die, shall he live again?"

On October 13, 1972, while driving along a usually deserted stretch of highway in the Santa Cruz Mountains, Herb spotted an old man staggering along the roadside. Herb stopped the car, lifted the hood, and asked the fellow to take a look at the engine—something seemed to be wrong. The man, Lawrence White, was obliging. Herb clubbed him over the head several times with a baseball bat and pulled the body off the side of the road. It was found in a few days and finally identified. Nobody got very excited about White's death; in fact, no one ever came to claim the body.

Eleven days later, Herb picked up a Cabrillo College coed, Mary Guilfoyle, who was hitchhiking. He stabbed her once in the chest and then in the back. She apparently died instantly. He drove up into the mountains and removed the body from the front seat of his '58 Chevy station wagon. There was no outcry about the disappearance of Mary Guilfoyle. Her body was not found for almost four months, and by then all that remained was the skeleton. The cause of death could not even be determined on the basis of the remaining evidence.

The first of Herb's killings that attracted attention in the press was the stabbing of a Catholic priest, Father Henri Tomei, in the confessional of St. Mary's Church in Los Gatos, about 15 miles from Santa Cruz. The killing occurred on All Souls Day, November 2, 1972, and appeared motiveless, although speculation went on for a week or so in the press about a "satanic or ritualistic cult killing."

For Herb, there was no relief in sight. Not only had voices told him to kill again, he was now receiving telepathic messages from victims who were "asking" to be killed or at least assuring him that it was all right; they "understood" the need for it. At his trial, Herb attempted to explain this phenomenon to the jury, saying:

> I, Herb Mullin, born April 18, 1947, was chosen as the designated leader of my generation by Professor Dr. Albert Einstein on April 18, 1955. . . . His hope probably was that the April 18th people would use his designation and its resulting power and social influence to guide, protect, or perfect the resources of our planet and universe. . . . *One man consenting to be*

murdered protects the millions of other human beings living in the cataclysmic earthquake/tidal area. For this reason, the designated hero/leader and associates have the responsibilities of getting enough people to commit suicide and/or consent to being murdered every day.

To Herb, in the context of his schizophrenic delusions, this made perfect sense—to the jury, it made no sense at all.

Herb decided it would be easier to continue with his mission if he had a gun. January was approaching, and this was going to be a crucial month for earthquakes. Many sacrifices might be required, particularly if others did not do their share.

On December 16, 1972, Herb walked into a store and asked to look at handguns. He selected a .22 caliber revolver and filled out the required form. He answered "No" to questions about previous arrests and mental hospitalizations, though this was actually unnecessary since under California law only "aliens, narcotics addicts, convicted felons, and minors" are prohibited from purchasing handguns. On December 22, 1972, having complied fully with the state gun laws, which require a five-day waiting period between purchase and delivery, the manager of the store handed Mullin his weapon.

During the next month Mullin seemed to be making a last-ditch effort to please his father and carry out his "mission" in a socially accepted context. He made repeated trips to the local Marine Corps recruiting office in an effort to enlist. The recruiting officer considered Herb "weird" and tried to discourage him. Herb had his father and various old family friends write letters of recommendation. He finally was allowed to take a physical examination at the Oakland Induction Center on January 15, 1973. He passed the exam, but was still turned down. Feeling rejected and ashamed, Herb moved out of the family home and into a one-room apartment in an old, run-down section of Santa Cruz, increasing his isolation. He was more and more preoccupied with his bizarre internal world.

On January 25, 1973, at about 9:30 a.m., Herb drove out Branciforte Drive, a long road extending from the city of Santa Cruz well up into a remote area of the Santa Cruz Mountains. (It is named for a settlement of ex-convicts, alcoholics, and other "undesirables" who were attracted to the area after the founding of the Santa Cruz Mission and settled nearby in 1797. Interestingly, within a few years the mission priest had been murdered and the settlers from Branciforte had robbed enough from the Santa Cruz Mission to discourage its expansion. The pueblo of Branciforte thrived, however, as smugglers found the hilly areas close by the ocean harbor a useful combination. Even today, small ships loaded with marijuana and other drugs have been known to unload their cargo at Santa Cruz for dispersal by "delivery personnel" who live in the remote hills and valleys of the Santa Cruz Mountains.)

Jim Gianera, the high school acquaintance-turned-drug-dealer, had been on Herb's mind lately. He believed that Gianera had given him marijuana in order to destroy his mind and to prevent him from being too powerful in his next life.

Herb knocked on the door of the small primitive cabin on Branciforte Drive where he thought Gianera lived. Kathy Francis, 29 years old, answered the door. Her husband was out of town and she wasn't expecting visitors. The cabin had no electricity and the only source of heat was a small stove which was out. As briefly as she could, she told the stranger at her door what he wanted to know—the Gianeras didn't live there anymore. They had moved the previous year, and she gave Mullin their Santa Cruz address. Kathy closed the door and heard the stranger drive away. Within the hour he was back. In the interval, he had shot and killed Jim Gianera, 25, and his wife, Joan, 21, at their home. Now he shot and killed Kathy Francis and her two young sons. No words were exchanged, but the telepathic messages had assured Herb that the victims knew they had to die and had accepted their fate.

An intensive investigation of these five killings was undertaken; within a week a long list of possible suspects was compiled by the Santa Cruz police and district attorney's office. Most of the suspects were people thought to have been involved in drug dealing with Jim Gianera or Bob Francis, Kathy's husband. Bob himself was considered a suspect initially, and I interviewed him at the request of the district attorney's office. He was able to establish that he was out of town on the day of the killings and provided me with the names of all conceivable "enemies" he could think of. Herbert Mullin was not on the list of suspects. A witness who lived down the hill from the Francis cabin reported to the police that he had seen a 1958 Chevrolet station wagon with a male driver heading up the hill the morning of the killings. He remembered the car because he used to have one like it, but he didn't recognize the driver and was not certain he could identify him if he saw him again.

Herb was beginning to have new thoughts about the source of the voices that seemed in control of him. Although they sounded like his father, perhaps they were from the devil. On January 30, 1973, he went to a Lutheran Church in Santa Cruz and talked to the pastor about the Lutheran faith. A few days later he returned to the church and sat in on a Bible group. Other members of the group recalled that he made them distinctly uncomfortable. His only remark during the meeting was, "Satan gets into people and makes them do things they don't want to."

A week later, Herb was hiking in the state park in Santa Cruz, in the same remote area from which he had been evicted for illegal camping a few years before. He came across a wood frame structure covered with sheets of plastic and entered the makeshift door. There were four teenage boys inside. "You must leave here immediately or I will report you—you are camping here illegally," Herb told them. They tried to talk him into leaving them alone and not reporting them. Herb pulled out his revolver. In his boyhood Herb had been trained in marksmanship, winning certificates from the National Rifle Association. Although the boys had a rifle in their makeshift tent-cabin, none had time to reach for it. Robert Spector, 18, Brian Card, 19, David Oliker, 18, and Mark Dreibelbis, 15, died instantly of gunshot wounds to the head, fired in rapid succession by the black-haired gruff stranger they had never seen before. Herb took the rifle and left.

On February 13, 1973, Herb awoke in his apartment and prepared to deliver a load of firewood to his parents' house. The "messages" were insistent and clear: "Before you deliver the wood I want you to kill me somebody."

Driving through town, Herb saw an older man working in the yard. He was Fred Perez, 72, someone Herb had never seen before in his life. A neighbor had just opened her living room drapes when she heard a "loud, sharp crack" that sounded like a shot. She went to her front porch and saw a 1958 blue and white station wagon driving off. There was a load of something bulky in the back and a young white male was driving. There was a red "STP" sticker on the right front door, she noted. She glanced across the street to the Perez house, saw someone lying on the ground face down, and suddenly realized what had happened. She called the police, reported the shooting, and described the station wagon she had seen. She was not able to give a clear description of the driver.

The description of the station wagon went out immediately to all police in the area. Within minutes the vehicle was sighted. Herbert Mullin was arrested en route to his parents' house with a load of firewood. He offered no resistance. At the trial, the district attorney cross-examined Herbert Mullin about the Perez killing:

Q: Who decided to kill Mr. Perez, Mr. Mullin?
A: Martin W. Mullin.
Q: You mean that you were instructed as to how to go about this killing, then, by the voice?

A: The thought I heard that morning was, "Don't deliver a stick of it [the firewood] until you kill somebody."

Q: Would it be fair to say that every decision made thereafter was yours?

A: I don't believe decisions were made. I think it was—a rock doesn't make a decision while it's falling, it just falls.

Four days after the killing of Mr. Perez, on February 17, Brian Card's older brother, Jeff, hiked up to see what his brother and his friends were doing. He was horrified at what he found and called the police. Bullets obtained at autopsy matched those from Mullin's .22 caliber revolver, already in the hands of the police. Four more counts of murder were added to the charges against Herbert W. Mullin.

Patient and Mass Murderer on Trial

The trial of Herbert Mullin began on July 30, 1973, in the Santa Cruz County Courthouse. Judge Charles S. Franich of the Superior Court, State of California, was on the bench. District Attorney Peter Chang was ill and his chief deputy, Chris Cottle, functioned as chief prosecutor for most of the trial. Jim Jackson, the colorful chief public defender who also defended John Linley Frazier and Edmund Kemper, represented Herbert Mullin. Since this trial demonstrated many of the problems inherent in insanity trials, I will discuss it further in Chapter 8.

Throughout the trial, both defense and prosecution agreed that Mullin had committed the killings for which he was charged and that he was seriously mentally ill. In fact, psychiatrists for the defense (of which I was one) and the prosecution were unanimous in their diagnosis: schizophrenia, paranoid type. The only disputed issue in the trial was the question of whether or not Mullin was *insane by legal standards*, that is, "Did he know right from wrong and did he understand the nature and quality of his acts?"

Public Defender Jackson, Mullin's counsel, argued that someone who kills 13 people for the reasons Herbert Mullin did must be insane. Chris Cottle told the jury that Mullin was "seriously mentally ill" but that Mullin knew and understood both that he was killing people and that killing was against the law. Therefore, he was sane within the legal definition.

Herb Mullin himself believed that he had no more control over his actions than a falling rock does over gravity. He believed that he had spared thousands of lives with his deeds—for there were no major earthquakes in California in 1973. When the jury returned with its verdict on August 20, he showed little interest. The jury found Herbert

W. Mullin legally sane, and guilty of eight counts of second-degree murder and two counts of first-degree murder (for the killings of James Gianera and Kathleen Francis). He had not been formally charged with the killings of Lawrence White, Mary Guilfoyle, or Father Tomei.

Jury Foreman Ken Springer wrote an open letter to Governor Reagan and the California legislature:

> None of this need ever have happened. . . . Five times prior to young Mr. Mullin's arrest he was entered into mental hospitals. Five times his illness was diagnosed. At least twice it was determined that his illness could cause danger to the lives of human beings. Yet, in January and February of this year he was free to take the lives of ten Santa Cruz residents. . . . Where do you think these mental patients went after their release from institutions? Do you suppose they went to costly private mental hospitals or . . . to the ghettos of our large cities and to the remote hills of Santa Cruz County?

The following year the legislature passed a bill prohibiting the Governor from closing any more state mental hospitals. Governor Reagan vetoed the bill but the legislature was able to override the veto. The hospitals already closed were not reopened, however, and the few remaining hospitals and community mental health facilities have become overcrowded. Coordination and communication between various psychiatric facilities and follow-up of discharged patients are often inadequate, as just seen.

In the case of Herb Mullin, the problem and the solution seemed self-evident. He was obviously mentally ill and dangerous. Had he been institutionalized and received continuous treatment, 13 killings might have been prevented. But how many killers are obviously mentally ill? And how many mentally ill persons are obviously dangerous? The next chapter deals with these relevant questions.

Not to be Reproduced by René Magritte.

CHAPTER SEVEN

PSYCHOLOGICAL STUDIES
OF MURDERERS

CULTURAL, SOCIAL, ECONOMIC, and other environmental factors have a bearing on the murder rate. But, if one wishes to understand the *act of killing*, the individual psychology of the murderer is the single most important area of study. One can generalize that the murder rate is high in the U.S. because guns are plentiful and readily available. But since few Americans take advantage of the ample gun supply in order to commit murder, such generalizations leave many unanswered questions: Why do specific individuals commit murder? What characteristics do they have in common, if any? Ultimately we must ask, can murderous behavior be predicted and prevented?

Later in this chapter I will describe a number of psychologically different types of murderers. The studies I shall refer to all involve human subjects. Although animal research has proved relevant to a variety of human behaviors such as learning, sexual behavior, and aggressive behavior, murder itself is a peculiarly human phenomenon. It is well established that other mammals, fishes, and birds rarely kill members of their own species. When animals kill, it is almost always for reasons that humans would call "justifiable homicide"—for instance, a male defending his mate and territory against an intruder, or a female defending her helpless young against predators (almost always from another species). Humans may kill for reasons (religious, political, etc.)

Murder and Madness • 83

for which there is no counterpart in the animal world. Much of man's destructive behavior (as well as creative behavior) is a product of the unique capabilities of the human brain; humans are not limited to inherited instincts or stereotyped patterns of behavior and individual differences among humans encompass a very wide range.

Yet, the fact that there are a variety of motives and psychological backgrounds in any human subgroup, including murderers, is a surprisingly recent observation. Earlier studies of murderers tended to look for general characteristics among all persons who had committed murder. The first systematic study of murderers was published in 1839 by a pioneer American psychiatrist, Dr. Isaac Ray.

Ray described two types of murderers: the *homicidal monomaniac* (the insane murderer) and the *criminal murderer* (the sane murderer). The differences between the two groups were primarily in method and motive for the killing and the subsequent behavior of the killer: ". . . with the criminal [murderer], murder is always a means for acomplishing some selfish object and is frequently accompanied by some other crime; whereas with the homicidal monomaniac, murder is the only object in view. . . ." He continued, "The criminal never sheds more blood than is necessary for the attainment of his object; the homicidal monomaniac often sacrifices all within his reach to the cravings of his murderous propensity." In the planning of the crime, the two groups again differ. "The criminal murderer lays plans for the execution of his designs . . . and when successful, makes every effort to avoid discovery." But the homicidal monomaniac, for the most part, "consults none of the usual conveniences of crime; he falls upon the object of his fury . . . and then voluntarily surrenders himself to the constituted authorities."

Ray noted that acts of homicidal insanity are generally preceded by striking peculiarities in the individual's conduct or character, which is not the case with the criminal murderer. He concluded, "A stronger contrast than is presented, in every respect, between the homicidal act of the real criminal and that of the monomaniac, can hardly be imagined; and yet we are obliged to acknowledge that men of learning and intelligence have often refused to acknowledge it."

In the 75 years subsequent to the work of Dr. Ray, a few studies were undertaken which focused on the physical (presumably genetic) characteristics of the murderer, disregarding such factors as the circumstances of the crime, or the relationship to the victim. For instance, in 1911, the Italian criminologist Cesare Lombroso concluded that murderers as a group were biologically degenerate and had bloodshot eyes, aquiline noses, curly black hair, strong jaws, big ears, thin lips, and menacing grins. In retrospect the studies of Ray and Lombroso may seem naïve, but they at least represent an attempt to understand murderers by means of direct observation and study rather than relying on abstract crime statistics.

Deterrents to the Psychological Study of Murderers

Considering both the seriousness of murder and the tremendous growth of psychological research over the past 50 years, it might seem odd that there has not been more effort expended to identify the types of people most likely to commit murder. However, there are a number of factors which impede or deter a behavioral scientist wishing to conduct a serious study of murderers. To begin with, such a study should ideally go beyond the analysis of a single case. But few research psychiatrists ever have access to large groups of murderers and therefore single-case studies of murderers predominate in the social science and psychiatric literature. There have been few studies of sizable samples of murderers. The difficulty of access to murderers is not simply due to the infrequency of murder. For instance, prior to conviction, an accused murderer's privilege against self-incrimination might be jeopardized by psychological probing of his personality, motives, or unconscious conflicts. After conviction, the murderers are often inaccessible in various maximum security prisons, or may have even been executed.

Finally, quite frankly, interviewing and analyzing suspected or convicted murderers in the grim atmosphere of a jail or prison cell is an unpleasant undertaking. Interviewing a client in the pleasant, familiar surroundings of one's private office, and collecting a fee for services rendered to a grateful patient is understandably more rewarding to most professionals than traveling to some distant correctional facility, waiting to be admitted and searched, and then being locked in a cell with a killer who may be less than pleased to see a "shrink." To be subsequently subjected to a grilling cross-examination by a zealous attorney at an insanity trial is, for many psychiatrists and psychologists, the most unpleasant experience of all.

Despite these deterrents, a limited number of firsthand studies have been conducted over the years that have shed some light on the psychology of murderers, revealing information which cannot be obtained by any means other than direct contact with the prisoner. A caveat is in order at this point, namely that the quantity and quality of data available from firsthand study of those who murder is still woefully deficient in contrast, for instance, to the sociological data available from police records. Sociology Professor Marvin Wolfgang was able to report his findings on 588 murder cases in Philadelphia after a 5-year study based on police files. It took Marvin Kahn, a professor of psychology at the University of Arizona, 7 years to accumulate a series of 43 murderers who could be studied by means of psychiatric examinations and psychological tests. In my own experience, I have been able to personally examine 40 murderers over the past 5 years. I have incorporated elements of two types of studies in my own work, the clinical and the psychometric, and will now describe the basic methods and findings of each.

Psychometric Studies of Murderers

Psychometric studies are those which rely exclusively or primarily on standardized psychological tests. Psychological tests were developed and became a popular research tool during the first half of the 20th century. The first standardized psychological test was the Stanford-Binet Intelligence Test. A 1926 study administered the IQ test to groups of criminals and tabulated the results according to type of offense. The study concluded, "In the case of each national group, the individuals committing crimes against property tend to rank higher in mental test than the individuals committing crimes against the person." Thieves in general were somewhat brighter than murderers in general.

Later studies have confirmed this early finding, but the slightly low *average* IQ among murderers is due to a few very retarded individuals in the population of murderers who bring down the overall average. Thus, it is misleading to think that most murderers are mentally dull; most are actually of average or above average intelligence (including those who are insane).

Projective Tests. Unlike IQ tests, which have "right or wrong" answers and absolute numerical scores, projective tests such as the Rorschach ("inkblot") Test have no wrong answers or final numerical scores. The data sought is not some ranking on a scale of one to 100, but rather an evaluation of the individual's subconscious or unconscious conflicts and motives. Subjects are shown vague and ambiguous stimuli in the form of inkblots (in the Rorschach Test), or pictures (in the Thematic Apperception Test, or TAT) and the subject is asked to describe what he or she "sees" in the inkblot or picture. The variety and content of the responses is believed to indirectly reveal aspects of the subject's personality and subconscious feelings.

Studies of murderers' responses to the TAT, in which the subject is asked to make up a story which explains what is going on in the picture, have found that many murderers perceive the figures in the pictures to be antisocial persons involved in impulsive, rebellious, or sadistic activities. For instance, a normal response to a picture of an older man and a teenage boy might involve a story about a father discussing a fishing trip with his son. However, a felony-murderer might perceive an experienced older criminal talking to the youth about stealing a car and traveling to Mexico, and a sadistic murderer might perceive a step-father about to beat the boy for coming home late from school.

Normal responses to the inkblots of the Rorschach Test often include the perception of human figures, benign animals, or inanimate objects: for instance, two women, two butterflies, or two trees. (Each inkblot consists of two mirror images.) Violent murderers are more likely to perceive two vicious tigers engaged in a bloody struggle; they are less likely to respond with perceptions of humans, particularly humans engaged in a rather passive social activity, such as conversation.

One summary of the findings of studies that use projective tests concludes that the impulsive, violent murderer "emerges as a personality characterized by egocentrism and a lack of emotional control. He can be described as an explosive, immature, hyperthymic [highly emotional] person who is unable to establish social contact. He displays a deficit of conscious control and a strong need for the immediate gratification of impulses."

Personality Inventories. There are other psychological tests, commonly known as personality inventories, which are somewhat more objective than projective tests, such as the Rorschach and TAT. These tests result in a personality "profile" and are preferred by some people who object to the subjective nature of the responses and scoring of the projective tests (despite the claim that subjective, spontaneous responses may be more revealing of the personality and that individual rating of the responses by an experienced psychometrist may be quite valid).

The Minnesota Multiphasic Personality Inventory (MMPI) is the best known and most widely used of the personality inventories. It has been demonstrated to be of value in screening large groups of individuals (e.g., Army recruits) for the presence of serious, potentially disabling personality disorders. The test consists of 550 true-false items, such as: "I am entirely self-confident," "I tire easily," "One should never trust his friends too much," "I have never done anything dangerous for the thrill of it," "Evil spirits possess me at times," etc. The items are scored in subgroups which comprise ten scales. The scales relate to personality characteristics or traits, such as depression, hypochondria, paranoia, hysteria, and social introversion. A score of 70 or more on any of the ten scales is considered abnormal. The overall *pattern* of scores on all the scales constitutes the "personality profile."

Psychologist Edwin Megargee has taken issue with the common generalization that violent individuals are invariably impulsive and uninhibited people with strong aggressive habits, acquired and maintained through social reinforcement in the home and subculture. He has been concerned with the findings that some of the most vicious murders are committed by persons previously described by friends and neighbors as mild-mannered, kind to children and animals, deeply religious, and "someone who wouldn't hurt a fly." Megargee and his associates therefore developed an MMPI scale that was specifically designed to assess conflicts between the *expression* and *inhibition* of aggressive impulses. Various investigators have applied Megargee's test to groups of murderers and have found that, using this scale, murderers can be separated into two personality types: the undercontrolled aggressive type, and the overcontrolled hostile type.

The *undercontrolled aggressive* group includes people who, because of the pattern of rewards and punishments in their development, never developed internalized taboos or inhibitions against aggressive behavior (Freudians would refer to this as a deficiency of superego with attendant failure to incorporate mainstream middle-class standards of behavior). Such persons lash out when provoked and show a lack of inhibition not only with regard to aggressive behavior, but with regard to the satisfaction of their acquisitive and sexual desires. Lacking internalized inhibitions, they are restrained primarily by external controls. The "undercontrolled aggressive" is similar to the "psychopathic" or "sociopathic" type and is apt to be a chronic criminal offender. Some people assume that the vast majority of murders are committed by persons of this personality type and therefore demand more police patrols in high crime rate areas and mandatory prison sentences for repeated offenders. What they are saying, in Megargee's terminology, is that external controls (police, prison) must be applied to persons lacking internal controls.

The *overcontrolled hostile* group includes people who have developed unusually strong internalized inhibitions against the expression of aggression in any form. Even socially approved outlets for anger, such as profanity or use of a punching bag, are found to be off-limits for such people. Their extreme inability to react angrily to frustration is said to lend to exploitation of the overcontrolled type by spouses, parents, employers, and associates. Megargee has hypothesized that in the absence of occasional outlets for the expression of hostility, aggressive impulses build up over a long period of time until a "breaking point" is reached, at which time the long-standing internal inhibiting mechanisms give way completely, and an act of unspeakable violence is committed by a person who never spoke a harsh word. Perhaps the prototype of the overcontrolled murderer is the long-suffering parent who suddenly kills all the children, the spouse, and then, overwhelmed by guilt, commits, or attempts to commit, suicide.

Although psychological tests can identify these personality types rather accurately and reliably, they cannot specifically identify "potential murderers."

Perhaps I can demonstrate the usefulness and limitations of psychological tests by example. Whereas the psychometric studies just described involved the testing of murderers after the commission of their crimes, the following data was obtained from psychological testing of Edmund Kemper at age 19, 4 years after he killed his grandparents, but 5 years before he committed a series of eight sadistic murders. The test results are consistent with the personality profile of the sadistic murderer described earlier, but they do not provide a basis for predicting with any degree of certainty that Kemper would kill in the future.

IQ testing given to Kemper included the TAT and the Rorschach. The following is Kemper's response to one of the TAT items—a picture of a boy and an older man:

> In this situation we've got a young man who's got problems, and his dad is counseling him . . . having a good heart-to-heart, man-to-man talk with him. [Recall that Kemper, in fact, had seen his father only briefly since he was 7 years old. When he was 13 Ed ran away from home to be with his father, but his father sent him back.] He wanted to follow in his father's footsteps, but then he had a lot of other interests he couldn't really follow if he did take a position in his father's corporation. . . . In the end, the son takes over the father's business completely and works at it for 5 years. [Is this prophetic of Ed's returning to live with his divorced mother? She often commented on the resemblance between Ed and his father: they had the same name, highly similar physical stature and appearance, and similar personalities.] He decides he really doesn't like that kind of work, it's holding him down, so he sells out and joins the Merchant Marine and goes tearing off around the world. In the end he was fairly successful in what he set out to do. [Unfortunately, at this point Kemper had told no one about his sadistic fantasies of killing women.] And the family just has to live with the fact that he has grown up and left. They have had feelings about "Where did we fail?" and "When didn't we provide what was needed?" So they worked to make sure that the other children didn't end up the same way.

Kemper typically responded to the Rorschach inkblots with images that were nonhuman and violent, such as "two bears running into each other," "alligator's jaws—his mouth is wide open," "oil fire in the distance, black smoke going up in the air, reflecting in water," "a trap-door with a spider at the bottom, sitting down in the hole waiting to snatch an insect." The testing psychologist's summary of the findings based on the Rorschach and TAT tests included the following observations:

> Emotionally, Mr. Kemper is somewhat immature and volatile. The prevailing mood is that of moderate depression accompanied by generalized anxiety. There is evidence of a rather substantial amount of latent hostility. . . . He gives the impression of a rather passive, dependent person rather than one who is overtly aggressive. The possibility of explosiveness is certainly evident, however.
> Mr. Kemper's view of himself and his abilities is primarily a pessimistic one. Many feelings of inadequacy emerge, especially during periods of conflict or other types of demanding situations. Self-confidence is low, and feelings of loneliness are frequently noted.

Kemper's responses to a personality inventory resulted in high scores on scales which revealed the following personality profile: "Intelligent, emotionally unstable, easily upset, shy, suspicious, self-opinionated, artless, apprehensive, noncritical, careless, follows own urges, tense, driven, overwrought, and fretful."

One can see that psychometric studies of someone like Edmund Kemper furnish revealing insights into personality and areas of emotional conflict. Such insights are useful in devising a treatment program for a patient, which is a primary function of psychological testing in a hospital or clinic. It should also be obvious, however, that these tests cannot go so far as to accurately predict whether or not a person is going to commit murder, or any other crime, at some future date. The tests were not devised for this purpose. Behavior in the distant future is never purely a function of personality type and subconscious conflicts; behavior involves a complex interaction between the *individual psyche* and the *environment*. For example, if Kemper had not been released from custody, he would not have had the opportunity to murder eight women. If he had not been paroled to the custody of his mother, he might have been less subject to tension and frustration and might have adjusted better to the outside world. Other contingencies are even more speculative, but it does appear that the easy access to guns, knives, and hitchhiking coeds greatly facilitated the execution of his crimes.

Clinical Studies of Murderers

The clinical method of study refers to a technique which relies on extensive interviews and observations of a client or patient by a trained clinician, usually a psychiatrist, but sometimes a clinical psychologist. Interviews involve extensive history-taking, including reconstruction of significant past events (e.g., divorce or death of parents, early sexual experiences) and associated emotional reactions. The clinician performs a mental status examination in order to diagnose the patient's present mental condition. This examination follows a rather systematic approach that involves selection from a number of standardized questions related to various mental functions (e.g., "What did you have for breakfast today?" to test memory for recent events). A complete examination also includes an appraisal of the patient's appearance, mannerisms, speech pattern, mood, level of consciousness, thought processes, thought content, perception, judgment, insight, and level of intelligence and maturity.

The examination may be supplemented by interviews with family members, review of past psychiatric records, school records, police records, and sometimes by specialized tests. These might include an EEG (electroencephalogram), or "brain wave" test, if epilepsy or brain damage is suspected; or a sodium amytal, or "truth serum," interview if amnesia is present.

Although the clinical method is more flexible and individualized in approach than the psychometric method, its validity is more variable because it relies more on the competence, experience, and conscientiousness of the examiner.

The best-known clinical study of murderers in the 20th century was reported by Dr. Manfred Guttmacher, a Baltimore psychiatrist. Dr. Guttmacher had spent over 25 years as medical advisor to the trial judges of Baltimore, during which time he examined 175 murderers. He presented his analysis of this series of cases in 1958 in a group of lectures dedicated to psychiatrist Isaac Ray. It was subsequently published in 1960 in a book, *The Mind of the Murderer*.

Guttmacher categorized the murderers into subgroups based primarily on his psychiatric diagnoses. The diagnoses were, in turn, primarily determined by clinical examinations. He found that 70 (40 percent) of the 175 murderers were seriously mentally ill and that 53 of these 70 suffered from some form of *psychosis*. Psychosis is a generic term which refers to a group of serious mental disorders in which the patient's mental functioning is sufficiently impaired so as to interfere grossly with the demands of ordinary life. Psychotics may be partially or completely out of touch with reality and may be unable to distinguish hallucinations and delusions from reality. Psychoses include such disorders as the various forms of schizophrenia and manic-depressive illness. Some psychotic conditions have a known organic cause such as chronic alcoholism, hyperthyroidism, or encephalitis. The term psychosis is only roughly synonymous with such older terms as madness and lunacy.

Several clinical studies of murderers have found a common distribution of diagnoses among those who are mentally ill. In every series of cases, including my own, the single most common diagnosis among mentally ill murderers is *paranoid schizophrenia*, the disorder exhibited by Herbert Mullin. A study of mentally ill murderers in New York found that 25 percent suffered from paranoid schizophrenia and an additional 24 percent suffered from some other form of schizophrenia or paranoia. A similar study in New Jersey found comparable figures of 28 percent with a diagnosis of paranoid schizophrenia and an additional 22 percent with diagnoses of other types of schizophrenia or paranoia. A Canadian study found 40 percent of mentally ill murderers suffering from paranoid schizophrenia and an additional 21 percent with other types of schizophrenia or paranoia.

One might ask what the point is in labeling these conditions or types of offenders. I think there are at least two obvious answers. First, as in the scientific study of any field, we need a useful way to classify what is being studied. Such classification systems usually begin with a simple approach and become more complex as knowledge of the field expands. The classification of murderers as *sane* or *insane* is as primitive as a classification system in biology which only discriminates between plants and animals. Classification systems provide a standard nomenclature that allows researchers in different places and at different times to compare findings and to generate new hypotheses for further study.

Second, in the field of psychiatry, diagnoses provide a basis for treatment and prognosis. Paranoid schizophrenia, for instance, is not usually a *curable* disorder, but it is *treatable*. Furthermore, the natural course of the disorder is known, and a psychiatrist can offer a prognosis based on this knowledge. He knows, for instance, that paranoid schizophrenia is characterized by acute psychotic episodes followed by periods of remission, during which many of the symptoms diminish or disappear completely. With *continuous* medical treatment, the frequency and duration of the acute psychotic episodes are considerably less.

A common tragedy seen in cases such as that of Herbert Mullin is that treatment of the psychotic patient is intermittent, at best. The patient may be hospitalized for a few weeks in a mental hospital during an episode of acute psychosis, but upon discharge from the hospital the patient may have no arrangements for follow-up care as an outpatient, or may attend a clinic for a while and then drop out. Without continuous treatment, the individual's condition deteriorates to the point of acute psychosis and he is then rehospitalized, only to repeat the same cycle.

Previous psychiatric hospitalization with subsequent lapse in treatment, as in the Mullin case, is typical of the histories of psychotic killers. In Guttmacher's study, a third of the psychotic killers had a history of previous psychiatric hospitalization, whereas only 3 percent of the nonpsychotic group had ever been institutionalized.

I cannot emphasize too strongly the well-established fact that mental patients, in general, are no more murderous than the population at large. While it should not be surprising to find that psychotic killers have been previously hospitalized for treatment of psychosis, *the incidence of psychosis among murderers is no greater than the incidence of psychosis in the total population.* Furthermore, the percentage of murderers among former mental patients is actually slightly *lower* than that among persons who have never been in a mental hospital. Crimes committed by the mentally ill tend to receive disproportionate publicity, which reinforces a widespread myth about mental illness and violence.

The high percentage of psychotics in a study like Guttmacher's is related to a selective phenomenon that is easily explained. A psychiatrist will be asked to examine, as a rule, only those defendants who are suspected by a lawyer or judge to be psychotic or otherwise mentally disturbed. In fact, in many jurisdictions, a psychiatric examination is required only when the defendant enters a formal plea of not guilty by reason of insanity, a statistically rare occurrence in the U.S.

Guttmacher went beyond the crude legal classification of "insane versus sane" defendants and described in clinical terms a variety of common subtypes of murderers. He made use of Freudian (psychoanalytic) theory and concepts in pointing out the effects of early childhood experiences on personality development and adult behavior, in describing the interaction of sexual and aggressive drives, and in explaining the emergence of powerful subconscious emotional conflicts and impulses while under the influence of alcohol. Bearing in mind that it is exceedingly difficult to do justice to the richness of psychoanalytic formulations in a brief synopsis and that many aspects of Freudian theory remain controversial or unproved, it is worthwhile to mention some of Guttmacher's categories of murderers since they are representative of the psychoanalytic approach that dominated American psychiatry during the first half of the 20th century.

The *normal murderer*, according to Guttmacher, is one who exhibits no marked psychopathology (i.e., suffers from no recognized mental disorder), but has not incorporated the values of parental figures sufficiently to develop an effective superego (conscience, internalized restraints). Such persons usually come from socially and economically disadvantaged families and have experienced significant emotional deprivation and inadequate nurturance in childhood. These factors lead to an inability to appreciate and identify with the ultimate deprivation of life brought on by the killing of another person and also result in a tendency toward feelings of extreme frustration. Frustration ultimately leads to aggression, and an extreme sense of frustration is most likely to lead to extreme aggression—a common sequence in the case of the normal murderer.

The *sociopathic murderer*, Guttmacher reported, usually has a physically cruel, rejecting father and perhaps a hysterical, seductive mother. The parents' marriage, if intact, is stormy, but often ends in divorce. The effects of cruelty on the small child are more serious than simple neglect. In retaliation, the sociopath inflicts cruelty on others and feels no guilt in doing so. The earliest objects of his cruelty are often animals. Adolescence is characterized by delinquent behavior, truancy, and running away from home. The sociopath exhibits no particular appreciation of laws or moral codes and will usually have an extensive criminal record involving a variety of offenses. The antisocial attitudes of the sociopath can be traced back to brutal, rejecting, inconsistent, and capriciously affectionate parents. In this context, Guttmacher noted: "A chief determinant in the adult's basic attitude toward the law, and authority in general, is his relationship to the first important disciplinary agent in his childhood."

The *alcoholic murderer*, when sober, is marginally capable of controlling the occasional antisocial and aggressive impulses that are common to every adult. Alcohol, however, functions as a "superego solvent" in these individuals, unleashing suppressed and repressed aggressive impulses. Furthermore, in the classic case of the male alcoholic murderer, continued excessive drinking leads to a loss of earning capacity and sexual potency—"two points of greatest vulnerability in the male." Feelings of low self-esteem follow, as well as a real or imagined loss of attention and love from the wife of the alcoholic. Pathological jealousy becomes apparent, often in the form of accusing the wife of sexual infidelity. Ultimately, he becomes convinced of the wife's infidelity (though the belief may be delusional) and, in an intoxicated state, he kills her.

The *avenging murderer* is one who kills in response to a sudden with-

The Pleasure Principle by René Magritte.

drawal of sexual interest by a spouse or lover. The victim is either the loved one or someone who is held dear by the loved one (a child). The latter instance is referred to as indirect or displaced aggression. When there is a coexistence of love and hate toward the same individual, the sudden withdrawal of the erotic elements of the relationship may produce an equally sudden release of the intense hatred and associated aggressive impulses. Abrupt desertion (or threatened desertion) by the sexual partner leads the rejected partner to avenge the perceived grievous wrong by violent means, often resulting in death.

Guttmacher also described other murderers such as the schizophrenic murderer and the sadistic murderer, but in these instances, the formulations are not substantially different from those I described earlier in the cases of Frazier and Kemper.

Psychoanalytically oriented studies have drawn attention to the importance of early childhood emotional experience on adult behavior. Indeed, it is now generally accepted that children who are neglected, treated brutally, inconsistently rewarded and punished, or made pawns in a bitter divorce or stormy marriage are more likely as adults to have emotional or drinking problems, or to exhibit antisocial behavior. Children who grow up in a stable family, receive emotional as well as physical nurturance as infants and small children, are rewarded consistently rather than capriciously, and when disciplined are punished without extreme physical brutality, are less likely to have these problems.

There are obvious ramifications here for child-rearing and child-care practices. Psychoanalytic formulations have not, however, found wide acceptance in the criminal justice system. One reason is that the legal system is based on an assumption that, with very rare exceptions, adults are solely responsible for their own behavior. Jurors, judges, probation officers, and prison personnel (as well as a number of psychologists and psychiatrists) are suspicious of Freudian theories which draw causal connections between childhood experiences and adult behavior. Furthermore, a few psychoanalysts have drawn far-reaching conclusions based on minimal data, which have seriously undermined their credibility. For instance, the Oedipal conflict is said to involve sexual feelings toward the mother which result in guilt feelings and fear that the father may castrate the powerless young boy as punishment for his incestuous desires. One analyst published an article in a professional journal in which he attempted to explain mass murder coupled with suicide as follows: "The increasing power of weapons for mass annihilation is related to the desire for power surpassing that of the father . . . [there is] increasing danger of self-annihilation due to the unconscious guilt related to the Oedipal conflict." As a practical matter, a psycho-dynamic formulation which concludes that someone has killed a parent because of an "unresolved Oedipus conflict and intense castration anxiety which originated at age 5" simply will not "sell" to a jury.

In 1974, Dr. Shervert Frazier, professor of psychiatry at Harvard, published a psychological study of 31 murderers in which he went beyond the traditional emphasis on personality assessment and the evaluation of early childhood experiences. In a number of the cases he studied, Frazier found that there was a *buildup state* or state of readiness, usually of several hours to several weeks duration. This state was present in all cases of preplanned or prearranged murder and involved physiological, psychological, and social factors. The physiological characteristics of the buildup state included restlessness, increased motor activity, and a high level of anxiety. In addition, some individuals experienced psychosomatic symptoms and a number reported sexual impotency. In women, symptoms of premenstrual tension were sometimes evident. (In fact, most violent crimes committed by women occur during the premenstrual phase of the menstrual cycle.) Common psychological characteristics were delusional thinking (often with a delusional fixation on the intended victim), low self-esteem, and depression. Social factors often included significant and repeated personally humiliating experiences which reinforced feelings of powerlessness and personal inadequacy.

During the state of readiness, Frazier explained, this type of murderer comes to the conclusion that he or she is trapped in a life situation from which no foreseeable outlet exists. A common finding in these individuals is a prior history of development of the buildup or readiness state which found release in an act of nonmurderous physical assault.

An interesting question, which remains unanswered at present, is whether or not an individual's crossing the threshold by committing a personal assault indicates that he may eventually murder. In my own study of murderers, the phenomena described by Dr. Frazier are not uncommon. Herbert Mullin, for instance, experienced this state of readiness on several occasions. The first time he experienced it, he was able to find temporary relief in a boxing match with his father. Subsequently, as he felt increasingly persecuted and became more delusional, he killed—first single victims and ultimately four at a time.

Murderers' Relationships to Their Victims

From my own study of 40 murderers, I have been able to discern a classification of murderers based on the type of victim they kill. It is my contention that the psychological profiles of murderers are similar if their victims are similar. Since there are a variety of victims, there are a variety of psychologically different murderers.

I believe that a common flaw in most of the psychological studies of murderers to date has been the tendency to assume that the single fact of having committed murder is a sufficient basis for identifying a class of people, murderers, who will be psychologically different from a control or comparison population of nonmurderers. Some investigators have separated sane and insane murderers for purposes of comparison, but in my experience, the "sane" group in particular is so heterogeneous that I would be suspicious of any reports of a single "killer personality" type or reports which purport to identify a small number of "personality profiles" which supposedly encompass all murderers. Guttmacher described 12 different profiles or "types" of murderers based on variations in the psychodynamics and psychopathology of the individuals he examined, and I doubt that he expected this classification to be exhaustive. In the remainder of this chapter I will set forth what I believe are meaningful psychological profiles that evidence themselves if one classifies murderers in subgroups according to type of victim.

Murderers of Children

Infanticide. The killing of infants or very young children is so different from other forms of murder that some countries (e.g., England) have statutes that make it a separate crime from other kinds of murder. I am not speaking here of *culturally sanctioned* infanticide, which has existed in times past in certain societies as a method of population control.

By infanticide, I am speaking of the killing of a baby in our society, an act which is legally and morally condemned. This type of killing is usually committed by a young mother; the victim is usually her first child. She is usually *not* under the influence of alcohol or drugs, does not use a weapon in the killing, does not have a criminal record or a history of psychiatric hospitalization, although she may have undergone counseling for marital difficulties or postpartum blues following the birth of her first child. These episodes are characterized by feelings of inadequacy, anxiety, feelings of neglect and fear of rejection by the husband, and seemingly inexplicable crying spells.

The postpartum blues usually occur within ten days of childbirth, last a few days, and go away spontaneously. In rare instances, about one in 1,000, a woman experiences a serious postpartum psychosis after childbirth. This can be a long-term psychiatric disorder and, without treatment, can endanger the life of both mother and child since the delusional thinking and severe depression which occur may foster homicidal and suicidal impulses. There is usually a buildup period, as described by Dr. Frazier, during which the woman ruminates about the method of killing, visualizes the child as dead, and considers her own suicide.

In the rarer instances of fathers killing infants, there is, in my experience, also a history of prior buildup states, from which the father finds release by beating the child or trying to stop the child's crying by holding its mouth and nose.

Susan A., a child murderer whom I interviewed, was a 25-year-old college graduate who strangled her 8-month-old daughter. She had been raised a devout Catholic and had no sexual experience prior to her marriage 3 years earlier. At first she was repulsed by the very idea of sexual relations and wished she had entered a convent instead of marrying. Her husband was a graduate student when they married, but subsequently dropped out of school and was unemployed. Susan taught school to support them until her pregnancy, at which time they separated and her family helped support her. Even before the birth of the baby, she felt very inadequate and was overly sensitive to remarks by friends and relatives, which she took to be severe criticisms of her shortcomings.

After the baby was born she began to feel that even strangers were making fun of her, and she developed delusional ideas about being possessed by demons. She began to have dreams in which she was attending her baby's funeral. Finally, she began to consider various methods of killing the baby and herself. She called a veterinarian to ask whether a certain insecticide was deadly and, if so, was the death quick, slow, or painful to an animal that consumed it. Finally she strangled the baby in its crib. She then composed a suicide note.

> I'm just sorry that each chance I've had, I've blown it—the guilt's too much now . . . if I lived, I'd just continue bringing sin into the world . . . it's better that she [the baby] go back into nothingness or be saved (as she is baptized) rather than grow up to be miserable and damned like me.

She then cut her wrists with a razor, drank a bottle of hydrogen peroxide, and turned on the gas oven. She was found alive, recovered, and was charged with murder.

Homicidal Children. During childhood sadistic and sociopathic killers often torture and kill animals. Although homicidal impulses may be present in some children, obvious practical factors such as limited physical strength and lack of access to lethal weapons tend to limit the opportunities for such an act. Children taught to use guns at an early age are usually closely supervised, although children in rural areas may be allowed more access to guns (with occasional fatal consequences, as when 15-year-old Edmund Kemper shot his grandparents on their farm). A homicidal child living in the city is less likely to have access to guns and therefore is limited to methods such as beating and strangling. This, in turn, tends to define the victim as a child small enough to be unable to defend itself or escape from such an attack. Again, a limiting factor exists, in that most small children are not left unattended or unsupervised for long. Sometimes the victim will be a younger sibling or a child for whom the older child is babysitting. In most such cases that I have studied the murderous child has displaced aggression, substituting the young victim for a parent who is the true object of the rage. For instance, a 15-year-old boy I studied wrote a letter to his father just before strangling his younger sister. The father had left the child's mother 7 years earlier and rarely visited the children. The boy wrote:

> Dad, I'm really sorry that I did this because I don't know if you really love Mary [the victim] and me. You didn't come to her [grammar school] graduation, that was a big thing to her, so now I'm not even going to graduate. . . . I wish all the kids would join the revolution and start killing off their parents.

Homicidal fathers. The victim of a homicidal father is most often a teenage son. The father, in such cases, is typically one who has been a marginally adequate husband and father and has experienced feelings of inferiority and frustration for a long time prior to the killing. Alcohol intoxication and guns are typically involved. There is usually no criminal record except possibly for offenses related to drinking (disorderly conduct or drunken driving). Neither is there likely to be a history of serious psychiatric illness or hospitalization. The personality may be described as "explosive." The killing usually occurs suddenly and impulsively, frequently in response to provocation by the victim in the form of insolent, defiant words, behavior, or gestures that are perceived as threatening, and are sometimes described as "the last straw."

James B., a homicidal father I interviewed, was a 46-year-old plumbing inspector in a sparsely populated rural county. He had managed to complete college with a degree in engineering some 20 years previously, but had never been able to obtain a job as a professional engineer. He had not done well in school, but blamed others for his difficulties. For instance, he felt that potential employers had rejected him because of his poor eyesight. He had other physical disabilities which he found frustrating, including chronic back pain resulting from an auto accident when he was in college. James also had problems with his family.

His oldest son, 19, had recently been arrested on a marijuana charge. His 15-year-old son, Bob, had been cutting school, and had also been driving the family car without permission (and without a driver's license). One Saturday, after working in the yard all morning, James B. sat down to watch television and had several stiff drinks. He heard a commotion upstairs and found that Bob had been teasing his 8-year-old sister by taking some candy from her. James usually refrained from physically punishing any of his children, but on one occasion 4 years earlier, in a similar situation when Bob had persisted in teasing his little sister, James picked him up and threw him down on his bed repeatedly. This time, when James told him to stop, Bob laughed at him. James then said, "There doesn't seem to be a way for both of us to live in this house," to which Bob replied, "You'd better leave then," laughing again. From this point on, James's mind became blank, but apparently he walked downstairs, got a gun which he kept loaded, returned to the bedroom, shot his son in the chest five times, and put the gun away. His next memory was of police arriving at the house. He had called the police, but by the time they arrived he had no memory of the killing or the call. He was charged with murder.

Murderers of Spouses or Lovers

Murder committed in the context of frustrated sexual passions, jealousy, and adultery is not limited to any particular socioeconomic, ethnic or other subculture. (A 1965 study by British psychiatrist R.R. Mowat found that morbid delusions of jealousy were the single most common psychological aspect of all murder and suicide in England.)

Probably the most common spouse-murderer is a husband who, after more than 5 years of marriage, begins to suspect that his wife is no longer in love with him. A buildup phase occurs during which his beliefs that the wife is being unfaithful to him become unshakable, despite evidence to the contrary. Often an assault or threat to kill the wife occurs some time prior to the actual homicide. The wife is usually genuinely frightened, but in a matter of weeks or months the fears subside and, if the earlier outburst led to separation, a reconciliation may occur, with hopes of forgiving and getting a new start. Not surprisingly, many of these murders occur in the bedroom.

One case in my study of 40 murderers was Marvin C., a 45-year-old master machinist, who had been married 8 years and had two children. Because Marvin developed bleeding ulcers, which resulted in several hospitalizations, high medical bills, extended periods out of work, and loss of income, his wife, Judy, went to work, first as a nurse's aide and later as a cocktail waitress, which paid better. Marvin ultimately returned to work, but began to drink heavily on weekends. Because of his illness and drinking, and her working at night, their sexual activity declined.

Marvin became increasingly critical of Judy. First he accused her of spending too much money on the children, then his accusations accelerated, and he became convinced that she was having numerous extramarital affairs. A week before he killed her he called her a whore and knocked her down; she responded by throwing an ashtray at him and calling the police. He moved into a motel. Five days later they had an emotional reunion in his motel room which included sexual relations that "seemed like old times." Marvin moved back into the home. Two days later, on a Sunday afternoon, he went to a neighborhood bar. On returning home at 5:00 p.m. he found that Judy was not there. He went back to the bar and did not return again until 11:00 p.m. at which time Judy was home. He accused her of drinking and having an affair with a divorced man who lived across the street, then he stormed through the house opening and slamming closet doors, shouting, "I know there's someone here." The children awoke and ran next door to a neighbor's house. Judy reached for the telephone in the kitchen, but Marvin jerked it from her hand. She grabbed a knife and ran to the bedroom. Marvin was unable to recall the subsequent events, but Judy died of internal bleeding caused by 15 stab wounds. Marvin was charged with murder.

Murderers of Acquaintances

Killers of casual acquaintances (as opposed to spouses or lovers) are most likely to be persons who grew up and lived in the "subculture of violence." The killer is usually a young adult male who, like many of his friends and acquaintances, regularly carries a lethal weapon (gun or knife) and uses it to maintain status among his peers and to "settle accounts" by direct physical action. There are a number of similarities in this mentality to the socially accepted practice of duels among upper-class males a few centuries ago as well as the showdown gunfight glamorized in Westerns.

In my study, Louis D. was a 21-year-old unmarried black who grew up in a predominantly black neighborhood in San Francisco. Although poor, Louis and his four siblings were better off than many of their neighbors. Both his father and mother worked while he was growing up. They had never been on welfare. He did fairly well in school, graduating from high school with a B average. He had been suspended once in the 11th grade for repeated truancy, and after graduation from high school he was arrested and convicted on two occasions for possession of marijuana. When he was 20 he moved to Oakland with his family, into a neighborhood that was tougher than what he was used to. At a party someone threatened him with a gun because he was dancing with the other man's girlfriend. Once three men pulled guns on him and accused him of stealing from them. On another occasion, a man who owed him money struck him in the mouth with the handle of a gun when Louis tried to collect the debt. During a period of a year there were five robberies in the small apartment house where he lived. Finally, Louis began carrying a .38 automatic which belonged to his father.

On a hot summer day in 1973, while Louis and two of his cousins were standing around outside a local liquor store, a drunken older man came by and accused Louis of throwing a pop bottle at him. Louis denied this, and an argument ensued. The older man pulled a knife and cut Louis on the hand before his cousins succeeded in pulling him away. The next day Louis heard that the man's son, Fred, whom Louis knew as a local drug dealer, was looking for him and had accused Louis of "jumping his father." Louis walked to a particular corner where he knew Fred would be and denied the accusations, insulting Fred's father in the process. Fred said he would kill Louis and reached in his pocket, whereupon Louis pulled his gun out first, and fired three shots while running backward. Two shots hit Fred and killed him. Louis was charged with murder.

Murderers of Strangers

Single victim homicides. The killing of a single stranger occurs most often in the course of the commission of some other crime, usually armed robbery. These homicides are designated as felony-murders.

Killers of an unknown person are usually men with extensive criminal records and personalities that fit the earlier description by Megargee of the *undercontrolled aggressive* type. They do not usually have a psychiatric history, but are often addicted to alcohol or other drugs.

In my study, Frank E. was a 21-year-old unmarried Mexican-American. He was the oldest of eight children and his parents had divorced when he was 14. He ran away from home to join his father, who told him, "I'll show you how to be a man." The father lived a nomadic existence, working in carnivals or on fishing boats, and occasionally committing armed robberies. When annoyed by Frank, which was fairly often, the father would beat his son with his fists, kick him, or whip him with his belt.

By age 16 Frank was in prison for armed robbery and served 2 years. Thereafter, he followed in his father's pattern, occasionally working, but most often supporting himself by stealing. At the age of 21, Frank was living in a small town, working with a traveling carnival and drinking heavily. Short of money, Frank and a buddy robbed a liquor store and pistol-whipped the elderly store owner badly before leaving. Seeing them drive away in haste, a policeman pulled them over to the side of a road on the edge of town. Frank hid his gun behind his back, got out of the car, and approached the policeman. When the policeman appeared to be reaching for his own gun, Frank shot and killed him. He was charged with murder.

Multiple victim homicides. The two most common types of killers of strangers, the schizophrenic and the sadist, have already been described. The schizophrenic kills victims in accordance with his paranoid delusions and hallucinations. His disorder is, in most cases, treatable. The sadist kills to achieve sexual pleasure and may choose victims with specific occupations or characteristics (e.g., prostitutes, or teachers, or brown-eyed college students, etc.). The sadist is the most likely to be a recidivist, and in most cases treatment is uncertain or ineffective.

Murderers of Public Figures

Assassins of political figures do not know their victims personally. Several persons who attempted to kill American Presidents have been examined and were found to be psychotic. Richard Lawrence was the first person to attempt to assassinate an American President. For 2 years prior to his firing two shots at Andrew Jackson on January 30, 1835, Lawrence labored under the delusion that he was King Richard III of England and that the U.S. government owed him large sums of money. Prior to shooting at President Jackson, he had accosted Vice President Martin Van Buren in the U.S. Capitol and even told him that Jackson would die if the money were not paid. At the trial following the assassination attempt, the prosecuting attorney for the District of Columbia, Francis Scott Key, agreed with the defense that, because of his incredible delusions, Lawrence was insane. Richard Lawrence was committed to a mental hospital, where he died in 1861.

The two best-known assassins of Presidents, John Wilkes Booth and Lee Harvey Oswald, died before any psychiatric examination could be performed. However, Oswald had been examined at age 13 by a psychiatrist who made a diagnosis of "incipient schizophrenia with strong paranoid overtones and potential dangerousness."

Killings by political terrorists are becoming more and more common in certain parts of the world, most notably Latin America and the

Middle East. This type of killing is almost unknown in the U.S. Although I have examined a few individuals who claimed their killings were "revolutionary acts," they were not political terrorists in the sense of being members of a political group or organization which supported the act as advancing some political goal.

The only well-documented episode of this sort in the U.S. was the attempted assassination in 1950 of President Harry S Truman by two members of the Puerto Rican Nationalist Party who were attempting to further the cause of complete independence for Puerto Rico by initiating a campaign of terrorism in the U.S. One was killed and one was wounded. There is no reason to assume such persons are mentally ill, but evidence exists that some persons who volunteer for high-risk missions are subconsciously suicidal.

The studies and case histories I have presented in this chapter demonstrate that there is no "typical psychological profile" of a murderer any more than there is a "typical crime of murder." Only by recognizing the *distinctive subtypes* of murder, murderers, and murder victims can one hope to understand the mental processes involved. Our legal system has not acknowledged these distinctions as yet. With regard to varieties and degrees of mental disturbance on the part of the murderer, the law uses a classification system as limited as Dr. Ray's "criminal" and "maniac" distinction. The law provides two possible categories—*sane* and *insane*. The next chapter describes the development and current status of the legal concept of insanity.

Courtroom sketch of Herbert Mullin testifying, by Don Juhlin.

CHAPTER EIGHT

INSANE KILLERS AND THE INSANITY TRIAL

THE PURPOSE OF AN INSANITY TRIAL, it has been said, is to "separate the mad from the bad." The law assumes a person is innocent until proven guilty, and the law also assumes that a person is sane until proven insane; that is, in a criminal trial, the burden of proving insanity lies with the defense, whereas the burden of proving guilt lies with the prosecution.

Insanity is not a psychiatric term. It is a legal category meant to encompass only those individuals who are so mentally incapacitated as to be unable to be held responsible for their actions and who require hospitalization rather than imprisonment. Contrary to popular opinion, insanity verdicts in murder trials in the U.S. are rare, occurring in only about two out of 100 cases. Interestingly, the comparable figure for insanity verdicts in homicide cases in England is 25 out of 100, and England uses the same legal standard for insanity as most of the U.S. jurisdictions. This striking difference does not mean that insanity is that much more common in England than in the United States. It does, however, indicate that in America there is a greater reluctance to believe that someone who kills is mad rather than bad. In fact, many people suspect that the insanity defense is a ruse employed by clever lawyers in collaboration with naïve psychiatrists to win an acquittal of an obviously guilty client. The popular novel *Anatomy of a Murder* described such a case; it adhered closely to the prevailing myths about the insanity "loophole" in the law and the ease with which criminals can pass through it. Although in recent years there have been various arguments in behalf of abolishing the insanity defense, the argument that this action would have any effect on the murder rate is, to me, particularly unconvincing. Recall, for instance, that England has a considerably lower murder rate than does the U.S., despite England's far more frequent insanity verdicts in murder trials.

Origins of the Insanity Controversy

Herbert Packer, the late Stanford Law School professor, wrote in his brilliant book *The Limits of the Criminal Sanction*, "There is no more hotly controverted issue in the criminal law than the question of whether, and, if so, to what extent and according to what criteria, individuals whose conduct would otherwise be criminal should be exculpated on the ground that they were suffering from mental disease or defect when they acted as they did." The origins of the controversial aspects of the insanity defense extend as far back as recorded history. At the heart of the controversy is the concept of *blame*—blame for causing harm to other people or their property. Since ancient times, the act of killing a fellow human has been the prototype crime, a wrongful act that cannot be excused, an act for which the perpetrator must be held accountable, and one which demands punishment. The Mosaic code, and other ancient systems of law, provided a penalty of death for the crime of murder in accordance with the principle of "an eye for an eye."

The need to blame and punish someone for an act as serious as killing is deeply rooted in the emotions. To attach blame or responsibility for an act of killing is *necessary, but not sufficient* for satisfying our sense of justice. For many people today, justice still requires punishment, and they further believe that the punishment should fit the crime. This is the concept of retribution, and murder has long been the archetype for retributive justice—that he who kills should pay with his own life. But, since the punishment of taking another life is totally irreversible, legal proceedings developed several thousand years ago in various cultures to protect the rights of the accused.

At times, the proceedings have been applied to seemingly ridiculous situations. For instance, in Europe during the Middle Ages, animals that killed humans were put on trial and were convicted of murder prior to being executed. At the other extreme, most notably during the reigns of certain absolute monarchs or dictators, persons have been summarily executed for murder, conspiracy, or treason, without the formality of either a trial or hearing. In American history, lynch mobs sometimes took the law into their hands and satisfied their emotional sense of justice by summary execution. One reason that a society based on laws attempts to provide a trial before punishment is simple and straight-forward: we want to make sure we have blamed the right person for the crime. There are various well-documented cases in the U.S. and elsewhere where an innocent person has been lynched. (Of course, there are also cases where a person has been mistakenly tried and convicted of murder, executed, and posthumously found to be innocent.)

Actually, in most murder cases it is obvious who the killer is. Consider the case of Jack Ruby. On a nationally televised news broadcast, millions of people saw Ruby shoot and kill Lee Harvey Oswald. Why was Jack Ruby tried for murder? Not to prove that he, in fact, killed Oswald. The trial focused primarily on Ruby's mental state at the time he shot Oswald—was he *sane* or *insane*? Legally, if a person is insane, he is not responsible (blameworthy) for his actions.

We have long since abandoned the medieval notion, for example, that a bear that kills a human should be held morally responsible for mur-der; we assume that the animal is incapable of moral intentions of good or evil and is unaware of the consequences of killing except, per-haps, in the sense that it may be "aware" that the person threatening its lair is no longer a menace. Similarly, the law has for some time held that an occasional person, because of a deranged or defective condition of the mind, is incapable of understanding or controlling his behavior to such an extent that he cannot be held morally or legally responsible for his actions any more than a wild animal. Society can rightly protect itself from such persons by locking them up in mental hospitals, but justice is not served by "blaming" them and "punishing" them for their actions. But since people, unlike animals, are only relieved of responsi-bility for their actions if they are so sick or deranged as to be determined legally insane, there must be persuasive evidence of mental illness or defect to lead to a verdict of insanity.

Thus, in Jack Ruby's trial, as in all insanity trials, a number of physi-cians were called as witnesses to offer medical opinions on the issue of insanity. Physicians usually find testifying in an insanity trial a frustrat-ing experience. A major source of the frustration is the all-or-nothing legal concept of sanity and insanity. Physicians view illness in shades of grey, rather than in the black-and-white categories typical of the law. There are various kinds of illnesses, and within each category, varying degrees of severity. Some mental disorders are acute (brief) and others chronic (long-term). The same mental illness may affect different people in different ways, and individuals respond differently to identical treatment. Furthermore, for many diseases—heart disease, stroke, cancer, and most forms of mental illness—the ultimate cause is unknown.

If you ask a doctor whether a given patient is sick or well, he will typically ask, "By what standard?" Similarly, for a doctor to determine whether the individual is *sane* or *insane*, there must be an established criterion or standard of sanity against which he can make this evaluation. There is no particular mental illness that can be equated with the term *insanity* any more than there is a specific physical illness that can be equated with the term *disability*. A psychiatric diagnosis is relevant but not sufficient for the determination of insanity in a criminal trial, just as a medical diagnosis is relevant but not sufficient for a determination of disability in a workmen's compensation hearing.

A *criterion* which allows a judge and jury to bridge the gap between a psychiatric diagnosis and a legal test of responsibility is required in order to reach a verdict in an insanity trial. However, a criterion that is both understandable and acceptable to psychiatrists, lawyers, and the general public (represented by the jury) has yet to be devised. In the next section, I will describe the various attempts to define insanity, from ancient times to the present.

Insanity Tests: Past and Present

Ancient Hebraic and ancient Greek law contain references to classes of people not generally considered responsible for their actions—namely lunatics and young children. Aristotle argued that the capacity of choice (called free will by later philosophers) is a prerequisite and therefore a test of moral (blameworthy) behavior. He concluded that because this capacity is lacking in animals, young children, and madmen, they ought not to be held morally responsible for their behavior.

The law of ancient Rome characterized an insane person as one who "does not know what he is doing" as the result of mental derangement. Although such persons were not to be punished for their behavior, they could be deprived of their freedom and other civil rights, such as the right to make contracts. During the reign of the Emperor Justinian in the sixth century A.D., a distinction between children and the insane was set forth. In terms of moral and legal responsibility for behavior, the child was described as "not very different from a madman"; but unlike the madman, a child might still be allowed certain civil rights and, with the passage of time, attain the status of a responsible citizen.

The wild beast test. English common law, from which most of our own criminal law is derived, recognized insanity as early as the 13th century. In 1278, King Edward I ordered the release of a man convicted of killing his daughter, because at the time of the killing he was "suffering from madness." The defendant was released to the custody of 12 men from his county who were charged with the responsibility of insuring that the man "shall not hereafter injure anyone." Shortly thereafter, during the reign of Edward II, the statute *De Prerogativa Regis* was passed, giving the King jurisdiction over "idiots and lunatics." *Idiots* were those born without understanding (mentally retarded), and *lunatics* were those suffering from madness acquired later in life (mentally ill). The test for lunacy became known as the "wild beast test." For a criminal defendant to be found insane, it had to be demonstrated that his mental abilities were no greater than those of a wild beast or brute. This formulation was first suggested by Henry de Bracton, a 13th century judge in the King's court, and was gradually accepted and applied during the following three centuries in England. The test was vague, but judges and juries were assumed to have a common sense understanding of the mentality of a "wild beast."

A more specific test for idiocy came into use during this same period. If a person could count 20 pence, state the name of his mother or father, or give his correct age, he was not, by legal standards, considered to be an idiot and could thus be held responsible for criminal acts.

Lucid intervals versus temporary insanity. In the early 17th century, Sir Edward Coke, a distinguished English jurist, introduced the concept of *lucid intervals*, arguing that some mentally unsound persons fluctuate between madness and sanity and that such persons ought to be held criminally responsible for acts committed during a "lucid interval" even though the person at other times might be quite mad and not responsible. Coke also described another side to this concept in his treatise *Institutes of the Laws of England*, in which he stated, "A lunatic that hath sometimes his understanding, and sometimes not . . . is called *non compos mentis*, so long as he hath not understanding [at the time of the crime]." This latter concept came to be known as *temporary insanity*, but was not widely accepted by the courts.

Child of fourteen test. Some 50 years after Coke, Sir Matthew Hale, chief justice of the Court of King's Bench, recognized and rejected the concept of "partial insanity." He noted that many criminals "are under a degree of partial insanity when they commit their offenses" but argued that only the "totally insane" could be relieved of responsibility for their actions. "Total insanity" he defined as a condition "where there is no free act of the will," and he stated that this condition prevails only "where there is a total defect of the understanding." As a guideline, Hale suggested that the best measure as to whether an individual has such a defect of understanding "is whether or not the accused hath yet ordinarily as great understanding as ordinarily a child of 14 years hath."

It is interesting how closely our criminal codes today follow the wording and concepts of centuries ago. For instance, the California Penal Code states: "All persons are capable of [i.e., responsible for] committing crimes except those belonging to the following classes: 1. Children, under the age of 14, in the absence of clear proof that at the time of committing the act charged against them, they knew its wrongfulness. 2. Idiots. 3. Lunatics and insane persons."

Knowledge of right or wrong test. During the 18th century the knowledge of wrongfulness, or the capacity to distinguish "good from evil," became the most commonly used test for criminal responsibility. In 1800, a famous case was argued that advanced the insanity concept somewhat beyond the idea of "a wild beast unable to know right from wrong." In May of 1800 a man named James Hadfield fired a shot at King George III as the king entered the royal box at Drury Lane Theatre in London. Hadfield had for some time suffered from a mental disorder which began while he was in the Army and had led to a medical discharge. Hadfield believed that God had commanded him to sacrifice himself for the world's salvation. Yet, Hadfield also believed that suicide was a mortal sin. He was aware that shooting *at* the king (attempted regicide) was a capital offense—treason. Hadfield's shot did not *hit* the king (nor was it intended to). He believed that this offense would ensure his sacrificial death, while avoiding suicide.

Hadfield was defended by the eloquent Lord Thomas Erskine, who succeeded in convincing the court of the importance of an aspect of certain mental disorders which previously had not been considered in insanity cases—the phenomenon of *delusional beliefs*.

The insane delusion test. Erskine argued that "delusion, when there is no frenzy or raving madness, is the true character of insanity . . . [his] disease, call it what you will, consists not merely in seeing with a prejudiced eye, or with odd and absurd peculiarities . . . but [his] whole reasoning and corresponding conduct, though governed by ordinary dictates of reason, proceed upon something which has no foundation or existence." Erskine argued, in effect, that although Hadfield knew that shooting at the king was a capital crime—indeed, that this awareness was his *motive* for the crime—his act was *based upon false beliefs*, delusions, which were not of his own making but rather were symptoms of his insanity, for which he was not responsible.

Erskine also introduced a concept which has been included in some of the most recent U.S. formulations of insanity—the so-called "product test." Erskine argued, "I must convince you, not only that the unhappy prisoner was a lunatic within my own definition of lunacy, but that *the act in question was the immediate, unqualified offspring [product] of the disease.*" Erskine's formulation of insanity followed this logic: If a person has a mental disease which leads to delusional beliefs and if that person then commits an act which results from the delusions, then the person should be found insane, whether or not he knew (as Hadfield did) that the act was considered a crime. Hadfield was found insane and was committed to an asylum. Erskine's view of insanity, however, was not widely adopted.

Just 12 years later, Lord Chief Justice Mansfield reverted to the earlier "knowledge of right and wrong" test. The case involved a defendant named John Bellingham, who suffered under the delusion that the English ambassador to Russia had failed to protect him from injuries he received there. In response to this and other delusions of persecution from government officials, Bellingham shot a treasury officer in Parliament, and then meekly surrendered. At the trial Chief Justice Mansfield offered this test of insanity: "Could the defendant distinguish good from evil, and did he have knowledge as to the crime he was committing?" Using this criterion, Bellingham was found sane and was executed one week later.

The irresistible impulse test. In 1840, a man named Edward Oxford fired a pistol at Queen Victoria. He had been known to be mentally ill for 18 years and appeared unable to comprehend the significance of what he had done, why he had done it, or why he was on trial. The trial judge suggested a test that presaged the concept of *irresistible impulse.* The jury was instructed that, "If this man was the agent of [a] controlling disease which he could not resist, he is entitled to acquittal." He was acquitted on grounds of insanity. Queen Victoria was enraged at the verdict.

The irresistible impulse test was never widely used in England, but it has received occasional support in the U.S. judiciary.* Justice Somerville of Alabama wrote in 1886: "The disease of insanity can so affect the mind as to subvert the freedom of the will, and thereby destroy the power of the victim to choose between right and wrong, although he perceives it." One of the arguments against the irresistible impulse test is that it undermines the doctrine of free will, a cornerstone of U.S. criminal law. In those few states where the test is applicable, the prosecution often makes light of the concept by referring to a hypothetical "policeman-at-the-elbow" situation. The typical line of questioning follows this pattern:

Prosecutor: Now doctor, you have stated that the defendant
                    was unable to control his behavior because of a

---

* The California Supreme Court recognized the irresistible impulse test for the first time in 1974. It may now be used in a defense of mitigation but not in an insanity defense in California.

	pathological urge or compulsion to do the act, is that correct?
Doctor:	Yes.
Prosecutor:	Now then, are you saying that this impulse was so strong and the defendant's ability to control his behavior so minimal that he would have committed this act even if a policeman were standing at his elbow at the time?
Doctor:	Well, that is hard to say. He probably would have postponed it until the policeman was gone, but he ultimately would have done it.
Prosecutor:	But you are admitting then, that he could have resisted the irresistible impulse!

Many insane persons would, in fact, be inhibited temporarily by a policeman's presence, but others would be oblivious. The issue is often irrelevant since it assumes, falsely, that sane persons who murder usually can and do attempt to avoid detection and punishment. This is most frequently not the case. (Jack Ruby, who was legally sane, was surrounded by policemen when he shot Lee Harvey Oswald.)

The McNaughton test. The insanity test presently used in most of the U.S. originated in England. A man named Daniel McNaughton shot and killed Edward Drummond, private secretary to the English Prime Minister Robert Peel, on January 20, 1843. McNaughton suffered from symptoms of paranoid schizophrenia, the most striking of which were his delusions of persecution. McNaughton had believed for some time that Sir Robert Peel had organized a government conspiracy to destroy him. In a statement made after his arrest he said, "The Tories . . . have compelled me to do this. They follow and persecute me wherever I go, and have entirely destroyed my peace of mind. They followed me to France, into Scotland, and all over England; in fact they follow me wherever I go. I cannot get no rest from them night or day. . . . I believe they have driven me into consumption. . . . They have accused me of crimes of which I am not guilty; they do everything in their power to harass and persecute me; in fact they wish to murder me. It can be proved by evidence. That's all I have to say."

The prosecution, to show evidence of premeditation, called a government employee, Edward Howe, who testified:

> I know the prisoner at the bar. I first saw him about a fortnight before the 20th January last. He was then standing at the top of the steps of the [Privy] Council Office, which is at

the corner of Downing Street. Sir Robert Peel's residence is in Privy Gardens, which is nearly opposite the end of Downing Street. Sir Robert Peel [McNaughton's intended victim—he mistook Drummond for Peel] at times walks up Downing Street to his official residence. . . .

On the 20th of January, between three and four o'clock, I again observed the prisoner standing at the Council Office steps, when I said, "You will excuse my taking the liberty, sir, but I belong to the office next door; you are a police officer, are you not?" To which he replied, "Yes," and I said, "I suppose, then, it is all right."

Within the hour, McNaughton had shot and killed Drummond near the spot described by Howe. Other witnesses testified that McNaughton was "a man of very sober habits," given to reading extracts from the Bible and studying anatomy. His landlady said, "He was very reserved in his manners. He avoided conversation with people. I never saw any companion with him. He was not in the habit of looking people in the face, but always hung his head down. He spoke quickly. . . . I attributed his sullenness to his difficulty in obtaining a situation." A gunmaker who had sold McNaughton two pistols and ammunition and knew him casually, testified that he observed "nothing remarkable in his conversation or manner."

McNaughton's attorney, Sir Alexander Cockburn, addressed the jury prior to calling the defense witnesses. He conceded the fatal shooting and said, "The defense of the accused will rest upon his mental condition at the time when the offense was committed." Cockburn explained that much of his case would involve expert medical testimony, since "a precise and accurate knowledge of this disease can only be acquired by those who have made it the subject of attention and experience, of long reflection, and of diligent investigation."

He quoted numerous authorities in his opening statement, including the observation of the celebrated Scottish jurist Baron Hume, who wrote,

> Although the [person] may have that vestige of reason which may enable him to answer in the general that murder is a crime, yet if he cannot distinguish his friend from his enemy, or a benefit from an injury, but conceive everything about him to be the reverse of what it really is, and mistake the illusions of his fancy for realities in respect of his own condition and that of others, those remains of intellect are of no use to him towards the governing of his actions, nor in enabling him to

form a judgment on any particular situation or conjunction of what is right or wrong with regard to it.

Finally, Cockburn promised the jury, "I am bound to show that the prisoner was acting under a delusion, and that the act sprung out of that delusion . . . and when I have done so, I shall be entitled to your verdict." Cockburn contested the prosecutor's statement to the jury that "the prisoner had some rationality, because in the ordinary relations of life he had manifested ordinary sagacity, and that on this account you must come to the conclusion that he was not insane on any point, and that the act with which he now stands charged was not the result of delusion." Cockburn countered, "I had thought that the many occasions upon which the matter had been discussed would have rendered such a doctrine as obsolete and exploded in a court of law as it is everywhere else." Cockburn's complaint about the prosecutor's view of the case is remarkably similar to the situation that occurs in insanity trials today. In fact, the arguments on both sides were the same in principle as those heard in the trials of John Linley Frazier, Herbert W. Mullin, and many other recent insanity cases.

The prosecutor's cross-examination of the defense psychiatrist, Dr. E. T. Monro, is also similar to the line of questioning used in insanity trials today:

Prosecutor:	Did you ask him [McNaughton] if he knew whom he fired at?
Doctor:	I am not quite certain. I think I asked the prisoner whom he fired at.
Prosecutor:	Did he not say he would not have fired if he had known that it was not Sir Robert Peel?
Doctor:	No, I think he did not. On this point he observed that the person at whom he fired gave him as he passed a scowling look. At that moment all the feelings of months and years rushed into his mind, and he thought that he could only obtain peace by shooting him.
Prosecutor:	Do you mean to say, Dr. Monro, that you could satisfy yourself as to a person's state of mind by merely going into a cell and putting questions to him?
Doctor:	In many instances I can.
Prosecutor:	Do you consider a person labouring under a morbid delusion of unsound mind?

Doctor:	I do.
Prosecutor:	Do you think insanity may exist without any morbid delusion?
Doctor:	Yes; a person may be imbecile . . . [also] a person may be of unsound mind, and yet be able to manage the usual affairs of life.
Prosecutor:	May insanity exist with a moral perception of right and wrong?
Doctor:	Yes, it is very common.
Prosecutor:	A person may have a delusion and know murder to be a crime?
Doctor:	If there existed antecedent symptoms I should consider the murder to be an overt act, the crowning piece of his insanity. But if he had stolen a 10-pound note it would not have tallied with his delusion.
Prosecutor:	But suppose he had stolen the [10-pound] note from one of his persecutors?
	[Court reporter's note: "Dr. Monro's answer was not heard owing to the laughter which followed the Solicitor General's observation."]

The jury found McNaughton "not guilty, on the ground of insanity." Queen Victoria was even more outraged than she had been over the verdict in the Oxford case. In fact, the general furor over the verdict led to an almost unprecedented procedure. The House of Lords passed a resolution ordering Chief Justice Tindal and his colleagues to appear before them prepared to answer specific questions regarding the doctrine of insanity in criminal trials. The result was the so-called "Mc-Naughton test" of insanity:

> To establish a defense on the ground of insanity, it must be clearly proved that, at the time of the committing of the act, the party was labouring under such a defect of reason, from disease of the mind, as to not know the nature and quality of the act he was doing, or, if he did know it, that he did not know he was doing what was wrong.

Many psychiatrists (myself included) have criticized the McNaughton test on grounds that it emphasizes only the *cognitive* aspects (*knowing* the nature of the act; *knowing* right from wrong) of mental disease while excluding the *emotional* and *volitional* aspects (the ability to choose and control one's course of action or behavior) of mental disorder.

Nevertheless, the McNaughton test is still the governing test for insanity in most of the U.S. and England, despite a number of attempts to modify it or eliminate it completely.

The Durham test. The best-known experiment with an alternate test of insanity resulted from a 1954 decision in the District of Columbia in the case of *Durham* v. *United States*. The Durham decision stated that "an accused is not criminally responsible if his unlawful act was the *product* of mental disease or mental defect." In a subsequent case in the same jurisdiction (District of Columbia), "mental disease or defect" was defined as "any abnormal condition of the mind which substantially affects *mental* or *emotional* processes and substantially affects behavior *controls.*" The Durham test attempted to include the volitional and emotional aspects of mental disease that critics complained were missing in the McNaughton test.

The Durham test remained in effect until 1972, at which time the same judge, Chief Judge David Bazelon, who had originally authored the Durham decision, rejected it in favor of a test proposed by the American Law Institute in its Model Penal Code.

Despite the fact that the Durham test was only in effect in the District of Columbia,* it was the subject of more controversy, criticism, praise, scholarly treatises, and vicious editorials than any development in the law on insanity since the McNaughton test, authored over 100 years earlier. One source of controversy was the definition of *mental disease.* Some psychiatrists and lawyers interpreted the definition narrowly to mean only serious conditions, such as schizophrenia or other psychoses. Others interpreted the term broadly to include persons with less severe neurotic symptoms, as well as debatable mental disease categories such as psychopath (also known as sociopath), drug addict, sexual deviate, and so forth. The other major source of controversy was the "product" aspect of the test. How can it be proven that a particular crime was *caused* by a disease? The symptoms of schizophrenia clearly influence the behavior of someone like Herbert Mullin, but it is difficult to *prove* a causal connection between Mullin's schizophrenia and his killing.

The Model Penal Code test. The Model Penal Code test that replaced Durham is *not*, in my opinion, a great improvement over the problems inherent in Durham. This test, now in use in several states as well as some federal jurisdictions, reads as follows:

 1. A person is not responsible for criminal conduct if at the

* The state of Maine adopted a modified version of the Durham test in 1965. Many other states considered and rejected it.

time of such conduct as a result of mental disease or defect he lacks substantial capacity either to appreciate the criminality of his conduct or to conform his conduct to the requirements of law.

2. As used in this Article, the terms "mental disease or defect" do not include an abnormality manifested only by repeated criminal or otherwise antisocial conduct.

A major change in this test involves the phrase "substantial capacity." Instead of a mental disease "causing a crime," as in the Durham test, we have a "mental disease affecting *capacity* . . . to appreciate . . . criminality or to conform . . . [one's] conduct." One obvious problem here is the vagueness of the term "capacity." It has no more meaning to a psychiatrist than the term "insanity," and in any given case the jury must decide what it means to them. A psychiatrist can testify as to the presence or absence of mental disease, but establishing a causal connection between mental disease and loss of "capacity" presents problems similar to those described earlier; the difficulties arise when one is asked to bridge the gap between a psychiatric diagnosis and a legal concept.

Having described briefly the historical and theoretical background of *insanity* as interpreted by law, I will now proceed to show how, from my own experience, this concept has been applied in the real world of an insanity trial.

The Workings of an Insanity Trial

The vast majority of criminal cases (over 90 percent in most jurisdictions) are settled without a jury trial. In particular, if the guilt of the accused seems evident, the prosecutor, in exchange for the defendant's plea of guilty, will make a deal with the defense attorney to drop some of the charges (e.g., two of three counts of burglary), lower the degree of the charge (e.g., from first- to second-degree robbery), or recommend to the judge a lighter penalty (e.g., 1 year in the county jail rather than 5 years in state prison). This is known as plea bargaining. A murder charge, however, is not so readily disposed of by such plea bargaining, especially if it is a highly publicized crime such as mass murder and there is strong public pressure for the ultimate penalty (the death penalty in some states, life imprisonment in others). A defense attorney might be derelict in his duty if he allowed his client to simply plead guilty to a charge that might carry with it the death penalty. In fact, in some criminal justice systems (e.g., U.S. military justice system) the law specifically *prevents* a defendant from pleading guilty to a capital crime. One reason for such a safeguard is that innocent people not uncommonly offer to plead guilty to certain crimes, particularly highly publicized crimes. Such persons are often mentally disturbed, guilt-ridden individuals. Others are extremely lonely persons seeking attention.

Insanity trials in murder cases often provoke considerable discussion and editorializing in the media. Some commentators believe that such trials are educative and function as a sort of "morality play," which helps a community to focus on issues of responsibility, morality, punishment, compassion, mercy, and so forth. However, press coverage of insanity trials at times tends to focus on the sensational aspects of the trial and evidence, rather than the more fundamental ethical and moral questions. During Edmund Kemper's trial, for example, some reporters were more interested in the alleged necrophilia and cannibalism than any other facet of the case.

One of the first issues the defense attorney must decide is which of three pleas the defendant should enter: (1) not guilty, (2) not guilty by reason of insanity, or (3) not guilty *and* not guilty by reason of insanity. If there does not appear to be significant evidence of insanity, the single plea of *not guilty* may be entered.* If there is significant evidence of insanity *and* significant evidence that the defendant committed the killing (e.g., eye witnesses, fingerprints, ballistics, etc.), the single plea of *not guilty by reason of insanity* may be entered. This plea is an admission of guilt; if the defendant is found sane by the jury, he will then automatically be sentenced to the prescribed penalty for murder. If there is some question as to guilt as well as sanity, a dual plea of *not guilty and not guilty by reason of insanity* will be entered.

If an insanity plea is entered, the judge appoints two "impartial" psychiatrists to examine the defendant and furnish written opinions (to the judge, the district attorney, and the defense attorney). In practice, court-appointed psychiatrists are often not impartial; in fact, some judges will appoint specific psychiatrists recommended by the prosecution and known to have almost "perfect" records of finding every defendant sane. Often such court-appointed psychiatrists have the same employer as the prosecutor (the state), for they are frequently on the staff of a state mental hospital or work for some government agency. Their opinions are filed with the court before the trial begins. If they find the defendant to be sane, they will subsequently be called as witnesses for the prosecution at the trial. Less often, a court-appointed psychiatrist may find a defendant insane, in which case he may be

---

* Evidence of mental impairment which falls short of insanity may sometimes be offered in the context of a "guilt trial." If such evidence is admissible, it may have the effect of negating the particular elements which distinguish murder from manslaughter, i.e., premeditation, deliberation, and "malice aforethought." This type of defense is based on a doctrine called "diminished responsibility" or "diminished capacity" which was developed in Scotland long ago. Limited variations of the "diminished capacity" defense are now in use in many states. California, since 1966, has had the most clearly developed concept of "diminished capacity." (It was set forth by the California Supreme Court in the case of *People* v. *Conley*.)

called as a witness for the defense. In any case, attorneys for the prosecution and defense will consult privately with as many potential psychiatric witnesses as necessary (when they can afford it) until they find one or two whose opinion they deem useful to their side. A psychiatrist may not be aware, when consulted, that the attorney has already consulted with a number of other psychiatrists who were rejected as possible witnesses because of their opinion on the case, their less-than-impressive professional qualifications, or other more personal characteristics that may appear to affect their credibility and therefore their persuasiveness to the jury.

The jury, of course, has no way of knowing how many psychiatrists may have seen the defendant or what the consensus would be among a significant number of experts had they also examined the defendant. In a given case, it is conceivable that 98 out of 100 psychiatrists would find a particular defendant insane. However, the prosecution will present the two who are willing to testify that the defendant is sane, and the defense budget typically cannot provide for more than two with the opposite opinion. It is no wonder, then, that jurors sometimes are confused and may comment after a trial that "the experts were evenly divided and since they couldn't agree, we disregarded their testimony."

Another misunderstanding which sometimes influences the jury's verdict in an insanity trial is the belief that a finding of *not guilty by reason of insanity* has the same practical effect as a finding of *not guilty*. In actual practice, the person found to be insane is sentenced for an "indeterminate" period (up to life) in a maximum security hospital. Furthermore, the doctors at the hospital do *not* have the authority to release such persons. If, at some future date (many years hence in most murder cases, never in some) the insane killer is deemed to be "restored to sanity" *and* "no longer dangerous," he may be sent back to court for a hearing before a judge on the question of sanity, but only a judge can release such a person from the hospital. (This procedure differs from that for a sane murderer, whose release date is determined by a parole board.)

Unfortunately, the law and the precedents in most jurisdictions prevent the psychiatrists from telling the jury these facts or discussing the defendant's prognosis with and without psychiatric treatment. These are issues that are often of great concern to jurors, but the insanity trial is concerned primarily with the defendant's *past* state of mind and behavior. What will happen to the defendant in the future if convicted or found insane is decided by the judge in accordance with various statutes. The rationale behind this procedure is that disposition (hospitalization or imprisonment) is a function of the judge, not the jury. The jury's function is that of a "trier of fact." Guilt, innocence, sanity, and insanity, are verdicts to be arrived at solely by consideration of the evidence (facts) presented at trial. Despite routine admonitions from the judge on this subject, jurors often do speculate about the disposition while they are reaching their verdict in the jury room.

In relatively rare cases, the trial testimony will focus primarily on the issue of insanity (responsibility) per se. Such was the case in the trial of Herbert Mullin, where psychiatrists on both sides agreed on the psychiatric diagnosis of paranoid schizophrenia. The disagreement centered on whether or not Mullin met the McNaughton standard for insanity. More typically, the prosecution will present witnesses who disagree with the psychiatric diagnosis as well as the insanity opinion of the defense witnesses. The testimony of the court-appointed prosecution witness (a state hospital psychiatrist) in the trial of John Linley Frazier is typical in this respect:

> Prosecutor: Do you have an opinion as to whether or not on October the 19th, 1970, he [Frazier] knew and understood the difference between right and wrong?
>
> Doctor: It is my opinion that he did indeed know the difference between right and wrong.
>
> Prosecutor: What kind of emotional problems, if any, did you find he had?
>
> Doctor: I found he was a sociopath.
>
> Prosecutor: What do you mean by that?
>
> Doctor: Well, a sociopath is an individual who doesn't profit from experience and who gets into trouble with the law.

On cross-examination the witness was presented with the official diagnostic manual used in the state hospitals and he conceded that the proper diagnostic term for the personality disorder he was describing was "anti-social personality."

> Public Defender: Now, the anti-social personality definition contains this statement:"A mere history of repeated legal and social offenses is not sufficient to justify this diagnosis." Are you aware of that?
>
> Doctor: Yes; I am aware of it.
>
> Defender: What else is there . . . upon which you base your statement that he is an anti-social personality or sociopath?

Doctor:	His arrogant intolerance of people. His setting his own rules. That's what got him into trouble with the law.
Defender:	Arrogant and intolerant are not words used in this diagnostic manual to describe an anti-social personality.
Doctor:	Well . . . it says they are grossly selfish, callous, irresponsible, impulsive, and unable to feel guilt, or to learn from experience and punishment . . . and that describes him.
Defender:	Give me an example of his selfishness.
Doctor:	Well, I think his attitude during the offense was pure selfishness.
Defender:	Upon what do you base that—that he killed somebody, therefore he's selfish?
Doctor:	Yes, it was in utter disregard of the others.
Defender:	That presumes something, doesn't it, that is that you know the workings of his brain at the time he killed someone, isn't that correct?
Doctor:	Well, I know the results.
Defender:	In this case, what about the killings themselves indicates selfishness?
Doctor:	He disregarded the feelings of his victims.
Defender:	Now, is he irresponsible?
Doctor:	Yes.
Defender:	What documentation for irresponsibility do you have?
Doctor:	Well, the massacre of five people is an irresponsible act.
Defender:	Would you say that all the information you have about irresponsibility was the massacre of five people?
Doctor:	I thought that was enough to come to that conclusion.

In effect, the doctor asserted that the crime itself was so "bad" it could only have been committed by a "bad" person. Jurors are inclined to agree, particularly in a case like Frazier's, in which the victims were highly respected members of the community and their children.

Disposition of the Defendant

In contrast to the detailed reporting and public interest that attends the insanity trial of a murderer, few people know about or are interested in what happens to the defendant after the trial (unless there is an execution), so long as he or she is locked up somewhere out of sight. One might expect that dramatically different consequences must be in store for the defendant who is found *insane* rather than *sane*, given the time, effort, and expense of an insanity trial. In truth, however, the end result for the defendant (assuming no death penalty) differs very little, regardless of the verdict. A finding of sanity for a murderer leads to many years, if not life, in prison; a finding of insanity for a murderer leads to many years, if not life, in a hospital that in most respects resembles a prison. Daniel McNaughton, after being acquitted of murder on grounds of insanity, spent the remaining 22 years of his life incarcerated in an institution for the criminally insane, where he received essentially no psychiatric treatment. Indeed, for the most part, the various institutions for the criminally insane in the U.S. today *offer no less in the way of punishment and no more in the way of professional treatment than do our prisons.* California is one of the few states that has a special treatment facility for the criminally insane (Atascadero State Hospital). The physical plant resembles a prison—stone walls and steel bars. But the staff includes psychiatrists, psychologists, social workers, and nurses. In most states, the facilities and staff for sane and insane alike provide "custodial care," but little else.

Abolish Insanity?

Since insanity is a legal construct rather than a psychiatric diagnosis, *insanity* could, in theory, be abolished legislatively. There have, in fact, been various efforts to abolish the insanity trial and insanity defense in recent years. Interestingly, the two major arguments in favor of abolishing insanity come from opposite ends of the political and philosophical spectrum. The argument from the right says that the insanity defense has been abused and has provided aid and comfort to the criminal by weakening the deterrent effect of mandatory punishment for those convicted of crimes. In other words, some persons who might not otherwise commit crimes may go ahead and murder, kidnap, rape, and steal so long as they have the belief that a good lawyer and psychiatrist can get them off with a plea of insanity. I have yet to meet a murderer who was inspired or encouraged to kill for this reason, or who would have refrained from killing if there were no insanity defense. Yet this aspect of the argument cannot be totally disproved. My personal judgment is that abolishing the insanity defense would not lower the murder rate. The assertion that the insanity defense is abused is readily rebuttable. Statistics quoted throughout this book show that the insanity defense is rarely used in the U.S., and is even more rarely "successful"—most jurors find such defendants legally *sane*.

The argument for abolishing insanity trials which comes more from the political left is based on the generally false assumption that methods and facilities for the treatment of the violent, mentally disturbed members of society *are available* or *could be made available*. The suggestion that accompanies this assumption is as follows: Psychiatrists should stay out of the adversary system; jury trials should be concerned only with establishing factual guilt (determining who fired the lethal shot); once the person who committed the harmful act has been identified, the jury should then be dismissed and a panel of experts should examine the defendant and recommend a disposition (psychiatric hospitalization, outpatient treatment, or imprisonment) to the judge. The variables this panel would consider would not be outmoded concepts like the McNaughton test, but variables such as *treatability* and *dangerousness*. "Moral guilt" as such would be an irrelevant consideration. If a person was found to be dangerous but suffering from a mental disease that could be treated, he would go to a hospital. If he was no longer dangerous but would nevertheless benefit from treatment, he might go to an outpatient clinic. If he was dangerous and did not suffer from any treatable disorder, he would go to prison.

The effect of this approach would be to increase the power of the "experts" in an area where there is, in fact, presently very little expertise. The deficiency of knowledge is not so pronounced in the area of diagnosis and treatment, although there is a serious shortage of professionals to make use of what is known. The serious deficiency of knowledge is in the area of predicting *dangerousness*, particularly on a long-term basis. The behavior of any human being 1, 5, or 10 years hence is contingent upon so many unknowable environmental factors that I doubt that we will *ever* have the ability to make highly accurate long-term predictions of dangerousness in most cases.

Rather than abolishing insanity and the insanity defense, my own opinion is that we should try to improve upon our present system—admittedly imperfect — and refine our criteria of legal insanity. Our criminal justice system is based on the belief that people can, generally, be blamed for their actions and should be punished when their actions are criminal. Yet it seems to me a necessary corollary of the principle of "responsibility for one's own actions" that, as with all rules of human behavior, there are bound to be exceptions, and that we should therefore have a mechanism such as the insanity trial for dealing with these exceptions. By so doing, we also provide an opportunity to periodically reeducate ourselves and reexamine the basic tenets of the system. This in itself may be a sufficient justification for insanity trials.

Proposals for Change

To adopt a new insanity test or abolish the insanity defense entirely would not dramatically affect the substance of a murder trial. The mental state of one who kills is almost always the crucial element in distinguishing murder from manslaughter, justifiable homicide, or excusable homicide. For this reason psychiatric testimony regarding the defendant's mental condition will continue to be relevant.

But we do need to improve the quality of presentation of such testimony. Courts should set higher standards for the qualification of expert witnesses. Currently almost all U.S. jurisdictions permit anyone with an M.D. degree to testify as a psychiatric expert. Some of these self-styled "experts" may have had not more than one course in psychiatry in medical school!

Jurors ought to be suspicious of "expert testimony" that consists of unnecessary, undefined professional jargon or circular reasoning (of the sort demonstrated earlier in this chapter: "Sociopaths are not insane. *Anyone* who kills five people *must* be irresponsible, callous, and selfish and therefore a sociopath and sane."). There is also substantial room for additional programs to train forensic psychiatrists who will be able to present coherent, relevant psychiatric testimony. Only a handful of such programs currently exist in the entire U.S. There is also a great need to educate potential jurors (the general public) about mental illness. The best-trained psychiatrist in the country cannot undo age-old stereotypes in the course of a few hours of trial testimony. The "wild beast" concept of mental illness is still commonly held, and unfortunately some jurors suspect malingering if the "insane" defendant is not screaming, drooling, biting, or throwing things during the trial.

Hospitals for the criminally insane do not differ much from prisons: both institutions tend to be located in geographically isolated, undesirable areas; the physical facilities tend to be old and poorly maintained; and staff salaries tend to be low. Small wonder that they have difficulty attracting high caliber staff and providing the same quality of psychiatric treatment available elsewhere. If the only purpose of the verdict of not guilty by reason of insanity is to provide a mechanism for locking up people who, although not blameworthy, are considered dangerous, then the present institutions are probably adequate. If, however, a finding of insanity is supposed to result in the defendant's receiving *treatment* in lieu of *punishment*, then we are falling far short of that goal. Society is justly concerned with problems of the economy and the environment, overpopulation and food shortages, war and threats of wars. But is the plight of insane killers so esoteric that it deserves the low priority it receives?

The plight of insane killers is, in fact, little worse than the plight of the hundreds of thousands of mentally ill persons in the United States who have never committed a crime but who also receive little more than custodial care in the grim surroundings of a state hospital. Many of these people would respond to antipsychotic medications and other forms of psychiatric treatment. However, the case history of Herbert ✳ Mullin is typical to the extent that it illustrates the haphazard and inadequate mental health services provided for chronically ill patients who cannot afford long-term private psychiatric treatment. His case also demonstrates a difficult dilemma for those concerned with civil liberties. If a person is identified as potentially dangerous, should society have the right to lock him up for what he *might* do? Frankly, given the potential for abuse of such power, I am reluctant to say that it should.

The Mullin trial also demonstrates the need for changes in the procedures of insanity trials. Present procedures do not sufficiently inhibit the jurors from arriving at a verdict influenced by or based upon their speculations about the availability and effectiveness of psychiatric treatment for the person who is found to be insane. Some psychiatrists have advocated a procedure in which jurors would only decide the issue of guilt or innocence; a panel of psychiatric experts would then decide the issue of insanity. I question this procedure on the grounds that insanity is a legal and moral issue, not simply a psychiatric one. On the other hand, I would support a procedure which *requires* the judge to consult with psychiatrists about the most appropriate disposition and treatment of someone who has been found insane. But an individualized treatment program which takes into account the needs and best interests of the patient and society *can only be implemented if the requisite facilities and competent staff are available.* Unless there is greater public demand for better mental health facilities, programs, and better trained personnel, the recommendations to the judge would be an exercise in frustration.

From the discussions in this book, I hope the reader's notions about murder and madness have been modified. Most murderers are not "mad," and very few "mad" persons commit murder. The "typical murderer" is a "typical human." His problems are our problems.

READER'S GUIDE

There is no up-to-date overview of patterns of murder in the U.S., a gap which this book hopes to bridge. Even basic statistics such as murder rates for the 20th century are not available in a single publication. Such statistics are listed in the *FBI Uniform Crime Reports*, published annually by the U.S. Government Printing Office in Washington, D.C. They contain detailed statistics for all major crimes in the previous year on a nationwide basis, with a further breakdown for each state as well as most cities and rural counties. I mention these volumes because much of the statistical data in this book is taken from them. But as they are composed primarily of tables and graphs rather than text, they would not make for "pleasurable reading." Nor do they attempt to provide information on long-term trends.

A number of books and articles are available on specialized topics relating to murder and madness, and I will mention them by general subject area. Of the 50 books and 100 articles I consulted in writing this book, I have selected those which are most likely to be available in a local library or bookstore, those which are most readable, and those which are the most accurate and important sources on a particular topic. Not all of the references that follow meet all three of these criteria by any means. Popular books about murder are often poorly written and of dubious accuracy, but are most accessible (e.g., the flurry of paperbacks about the Manson "family" murders which appeared in bookstores everywhere a few years ago). On the other hand, some of the best-documented, most insightful books in the field are not available in most bookstores and are sometimes less than easy to read because of technical jargon and complicated statistical analyses. Most of the books I will mention should be available in large public libraries. Articles from professional journals are most likely to be found in a college, university, medical, or legal library. However, many local public libraries will obtain a journal or book for you through the national interlibrary loan service if it is not in a local library. (There is usually a small fee charged for this service, but it greatly broadens the range of reading material available.)

Celebrated Murder Cases

Some interesting nonfiction books about murder have been based on actual case histories and trials. Many include psychological analyses of the murderers as presented by psychiatric witnesses in the course of the trial. *Before I Kill More* by Lucy Freeman (New York: Pocket Books, Inc., 1955) is the story of William Heirens, the Chicago mass murderer mentioned in Chapter 5. The book is well written and draws heavily on actual reports and interviews with psychiatrists, police, and others involved in the case. The author's personal interpretations are a bit too heavily Freudian for my own tastes, but the book is generally objective and carefully researched. *The Boston Strangler* by Gerald Frank (New York: The New American Library, 1967) was a best-seller which the New York Times called "compulsively readable" and "continuously engrossing." It describes the bizarre history and activities of the accused Boston Strangler, Albert De Salvo, as well as the tactics of his controversial attorney, F. Lee Bailey. A technically fictional, but basically accurate account of the Leopold and Loeb trial can be found in *Compulsion* by Meyer Levin (New York: Pocket Books, Inc., 1958). Clarence Darrow was attorney for the defense in this trial which was also notable for its unprecedented use of psychiatric testimony. One of the defendants in this celebrated case wrote an autobiography many years later while in prison. The book is *Life Plus 99 Years* by Nathan Leopold (Garden City, New York: Doubleday, 1958). Two recent paperback books provide more details about the Santa Cruz mass murderers (John Frazier, Edmund Kemper, and Herbert Mullin) and their victims, but little in the way of analysis or insight. They are: *Urge to Kill* by Ward Damio (New York: Pinnacle Books, 1974) and *Sacrifice Unto Me* by Don West (New York: Pyramid Books, 1974).

One of the best books written about a murder trial and insanity defense is *The Trial of Jack Ruby* by John Kaplan and Jon Waltz (New York: Macmillan, 1965). Kaplan, a Stanford Law School professor, provides legal commentary about the actual trial proceedings as well as the tactics of defense attorney Melvin Belli and other attorneys involved in the case.

Murder and Society

The most prolific scientific writer in the area of social factors and murder is sociologist Marvin Wolfgang of the University of Pennsylvania. A study of patterns of murder in Philadelphia, a classic in its field, was published in his *Patterns of Criminal Homicide* (Philadelphia: University of Pennsylvania Press, 1958). The theory of violent subcultures is set forth in his book *The Subculture of Violence* (London: Tavi-stock Publications, 1967). It contains a number of interesting descriptions of the history and practices of violent subcultures around the world (e.g., the Barbaracino Code of Sardinia, the Besa tradition of vendetta in Albania, and the "Criminal Tribes" of India). A collection of articles by a group of prominent sociologists and psychiatrists, edited by Wolf-gang, can be found in *Studies in Homicide* (New York: Harper & Row, 1967).

The basic data for the theory of internal and external restraints described in Chapter 2 is found in *Suicide and Homicide* by Andrew F. Henry and James F. Short Jr. (Glencoe, Illinois: The Free Press, 1954). This book is not light reading, but contains a wealth of data and a number of provocative hypotheses relating murder and suicide to such factors as social status and the business cycle.

Historical Background

Two books are particularly noteworthy for their descriptions of murder and other violent crimes in the context of 19th- and early 20th-century U.S. history. *Homicide in the United States* by H. C. Brearley (Montclair, New Jersey: Patterson Smith, 1969) is a well-written study of murder in the United States up to 1930. It contains a number of interesting vignettes about the presumed causes of murder in the U.S. 50 years ago and more.

A fascinating book about the development of Southern culture and traditions is *The Militant South 1800-1861* by John Hope Franklin (Cambridge, Massachusetts: Harvard University Press, 1956). Franklin is one of the country's leading historians and writes better than most novelists.

Insanity and Criminal Justice

A scholarly and readable discussion of the concepts introduced in Chapter 8 can be found in *The Insanity Defense* by Abraham S. Gold-stein (New Haven, Connecticut: Yale University Press, 1967). Goldstein is a professor at Yale Law School. The book is available in paperback. Two provocative books which are critical of our criminal justice system are *The Crime of Punishment* by Karl Menninger, M.D. (New York: Viking Press, 1966) and *Crime in America: Observations on Its Nature, Causes, Prevention, and Control* by Ramsey Clark (New York: Simon & Schuster, 1970). Heavier reading, but worth it for the reader who seeks to understand the theory as well as practice of our criminal justice system, is *The Limits of the Criminal Sanction* by Herbert L. Packer (Stanford, California: Stanford University Press, 1968). The question of the death penalty most often arises in murder cases and the many facets of this controversial subject are discussed by a number of authors in *The Death Penalty in America* edited by Hugo O. Bedau (New York: Anchor Books, 1967).

Articles on Specialized Topics

For the reader who may wish to pursue the professional literature on a specific topic that may have been covered only briefly in this book, I have included a list of articles. Each article has a bibliography which provides further references on the topic. The titles are basically self-explanatory.

Murder: Cross-Cultural Studies

Walter D. Connor, "Criminal Homicide, U.S.S.R./U.S.A.: Reflections of Soviet Data in a Comparative Framework," *Journal of Criminal Law and Criminology*, vol. 64, p. 111, 1973.

David Lester, "External Restraints, Suicide, and Homicide: Comparison of Norway and France," *Perceptual and Motor Skills*, vol. 36, p. 646, 1973.

Stuart Palmer, "Murder and Suicide in Forty Non-Literate Societies," *Journal of Criminal Law, Criminology and Police Science*, vol. 56, p. 320, 1965.

Kaare Svalastoga, "Homicide and Social Contact in Denmark," *American Journal of Sociology*, vol. 62, p. 37, 1956.

M. Wong and K. Singer, "Abnormal Homicide in Hong Kong," *British Journal of Psychiatry*, vol. 123, p. 295, 1973.

Arthur L. Wood, "A Socio-Structural Analysis of Murder, Suicide, and Economic Crime in Ceylon," *American Sociological Review*, vol. 26, p. 745, 1961.

Murder and Suicide

Martin Gold, "Suicide, Homicide, and the Socialization of Aggression," *American Journal of Sociology*, vol. 63, p. 651, 1949.

Michael Lalli and Stanley H. Turner, "Suicide and Homicide: A Comparative Analysis by Race and Occupational Levels," *Journal of Criminal Law, Criminology and Police Science*, vol. 59, p. 191, 1968.

David Lester, "Suicide and Homicide: Bias in the Examination of the Relationship Between Suicide and Homicide Rates," *Social Psychiatry*, vol. 6, p. 80, 1970.

Thomas F. Pettigrew and Rosalind Barclay Spier, "The Ecological Structure of Negro Homicide," *American Journal of Sociology*, vol. 47, p. 621, 1962.

Austin L. Porterfield, "Indices of Suicide and Homicide by States and Cities: Some Southern–Non-Southern Contrasts with Implications for Research," *American Sociological Review*, p. 481, 1949.

John Shelton Reed, "To Live—and Die—in Dixie: A Contribution to the Study of Southern Violence," *Political Science Quarterly*, vol. 86, p. 429, 1971.

Biological Bases of Aggression

Barbara J. Culliton, "Patients' Rights: Harvard is Site of Battle over X and Y Chromosomes," *Science*, vol. 186, p. 715, 1974.

Donald T. Lunde and David A. Hamburg, "Techniques for Assessing the Effects of Sex Hormones on Affect, Arousal, and Aggression in Humans," *Recent Progress in Hormone Research*, vol. 28, p. 627, 1972.

Victim-Precipitated Murder

Marvin E. Wolfgang, "Victim-Precipitated Criminal Homicide," *Journal of Criminal Law, Criminology and Police Science*, vol. 48, p. 1, 1957.

Marvin E. Wolfgang, "Suicide by Means of Victim-Precipitated Homicide," *Journal of Clinical and Experimental Psychopathology*, vol. 20, p. 335, 1959.

Murder and Mental Illness

John Lanzkron, M.D., "Murder and Insanity: A Survey," *American Journal of Psychiatry*, vol. 119, p. 754, 1963.

C.K. McKnight, M.D., J.W. Mohr, R.E. Quinsey, and J. Erochko, "Mental Illness and Homicide," *Canadian Psychiatric Association Journal*, vol. 11, p. 91, 1966.

Murder and Alcohol

Donald W. Goodwin, M.D., "Alcohol in Suicide and Homicide," *Quarterly Journal of Studies in Alcoholism*, vol. 34, p. 144, 1973.

L.C. le Roux and L.S. Smith, "Violent Deaths and Alcoholic Intoxication," *Journal of Forensic Medicine*, vol. 11, p. 131, 1964.

Marvin E. Wolfgang and Rolf B. Strohm, "The Relationship Between Alcohol and Criminal Homicide in New York City," *New York State Journal of Medicine*, p. 2154, September 1, 1972.

Murder and Guns

Judge George Edwards, "Murder and Gun Control," *American Journal of Psychiatry*, vol. 827, p. 811, 1972.

George D. Newton and Franklin Zimring, "Firearms and Violence in American Life," National Commission on the Causes and Prevention of Violence, 1969 (Washington, D.C., U.S. Government Printing Office).

Stefan A. Pasternack, M.D., "The American Connection: Handguns and Homicide," *Medical Annals of the District of Columbia*, vol. 42, p. 369, 1973.

Steven Thomas Seitz, "Firearms, Homicides, and Gun Control Effectiveness," *Law and Society Review*, vol. 6, p. 595, 1972.

Franklin Zimring, "Is Gun Control Likely to Reduce Violent Killings?" *University of Chicago Law Review*, vol. 35, p. 721, 1967.

Sex Murders

Robert P. Brittain, "The Sadistic Murderer," *Medical Science and the Law*, vol. 10, p. 198, 1970.

Foster Kennedy, M.D., Harry R. Hoffman, M.D., and William H. Haines, M.D., "A Study of William Heirens," *American Journal of Psychiatry*, vol. 104, p. 113, 1947.

Eugene Revitch, M.D., "Sex Murder and the Potential Sex Murderer," *Diseases of the Nervous System*, vol. 26, p. 640, 1965.

Mass Murderers

Ralph S. Banay, M.D., "Psychology of a Mass Murderer," *Journal of Forensic Science*, vol. 1, p. 1, 1956.

Eric Berne, M.D., "Cultural Aspects of a Multiple Murder," *Psychiatry Quarterly Survey*, vol. 24, p. 250, 1950.

Hilde Bruch, M.D., "Mass Murder: The Wagner Case," *American Journal of Psychiatry*, vol. 124, p. 147, 1967.

James A.V. Galvin, M.D., and John M. MacDonald, M.D., "Psychiatric Study of a Mass Murderer," *American Journal of Psychiatry*, vol. 115, p. 1057, 1959.

Marvin W. Kahn, "Psychological Test Study of a Mass Murderer," *Journal of Projective Techniques*, vol. 24, p. 148, 1960.

Murder: Psychological Factors

R. Blackburn, "Personality in Relation to Extreme Aggression in Psychiatric Offenders," *British Journal of Psychiatry*, vol. 114, p. 821, 1968.

R. Blackburn, "Personality Types Among Abnormal Homicides," *British Journal of Criminology*, vol. 11, p. 14, 1971.

Marvin W. Kahn, "Murderers Who Plead Insanity: A Descriptive Factor-Analytic Study of Personality, Social, and History Variables," *Genetic Psychology Monographs*, vol. 84, p. 275, 1971.

Edwin I. Megargee, Patrick E. Cook, and Gerald A. Mendelsohn, "Development and Validation of an MMPI Scale of Assaultiveness in Overcontrolled Individuals," *Journal of Abnormal Psychology*, vol. 72, p. 519, 1967.

William C. Perdue and David Lester, "Temperamentally Suited to Kill: The Personality of Murderers," *Corrective and Social Psychiatry and Journal of Behavioral Technology, Methods and Therapy*, vol. 20, p. 13, 1974.

W.C. White Jr., W. George McAddo, and Edwin I. Megargee, "Personality Factors Associated with Over and Undercontrolled Offenders," *Journal of Personality Assessment*, vol. 37, p. 473, 1973.

INDEX

My Lai, 61
Mythology of murder, 2-3, 6

Narcotics and murder, 45
National Rifle Association, 79
Natural disasters and murder, 64
Necrophilia, 120
Non compos mentis, 111

Oedipal conflict, 96-97
Ohta, Dr. Victor M., 49
Oliker, David, 79
Oswald, Lee Harvey, 15, 104, 109, 114
Overcontrolled hostility, 88
Oxford, Edward, 113

Packer, Herbert L., 108, 129, 130
Paranoid schizophrenia, 63, 92, 104
    early manifestations of, 68
    and mass murder, 35, 48-52
    treatment for, 52
Parents
    of criminals, 18
    homicidal, 99-101
    of sociopaths, 94, 96
Pascal, Pat, 49
Patterns of Criminal Homicide, 129
Peel, Sir Robert, 114-115
Penal Code, California, 112
People's Republic of China, 43
Perez, Fred, 79
Personality inventory, 87-90
Pettigrew, Thomas, 20
Physical characteristics of killers, 84
Plea bargaining, 119
Police records of homicide partici-
    pants, 10
Political extremist concepts, 124-125
Political terrorists, 104-105
Population density and murder rate,
    7
Porterfield, Austin, 23
Premeditation, 4
Premenstrual tension, 97
Press, attitude of, 120
"Product test," 112-113
Prohibition, 14, 16
    murder rate during, 32
Projective test conclusions, 87-90

Psychiatric circular reasoning, 122-
    123
Psychiatric ghetto, 75
Psychiatrists
    forensic training of, 126
    and insanity trials, 85
    theory of suicide, 23
Psychologists and insanity trials, 85
Psychology
    of mass murder, 60-61
    of murder, 60-61, 83
Psychometric studies, 86
Psychosis
    and drugs, 51
    incidence of, 91-93
    and religious fanaticism, 50
Public mental health fiasco, Cali-
    fornia, 75
Public school system and crime rate,
    16
Punishment
    as deterrent, 10, 11
    or treatment, 122-123

Race
    and murder, 5, 40
    and weapons, 6
Rais, Gilles de, 59-60
Rape and murder, 5
Ray, Dr. Isaac, 84, 91, 105
Reagan, Ronald, 74-75, 81
Redfield, Horace V., 20-21
Reform of criminal codes, 124-127
Regional statistics, 6-7
Rehabilitation, 1-2
Religion
    and delusion, 50, 67-69, 71
    and mortality rates, 25
    of murderers, 40-41
    of suicides, 40-41
Religious fanaticism, 50, 64, 71
Research problems, 85-86
Responsibility, 109, 126
Retribution murder, 60
Right or wrong test, 112
Right to bear arms, 28
Rorschach test, 86, 87, 89
Ruby, Jack, 109, 114

Sacrifice Unto Me, 129

Courtroom sketch, by Don Juhlin.

ABOUT THE AUTHOR

Dr. Donald Lunde is a psychiatrist who obviously enjoys interdisciplinary teaching. He is familiar to Stanford undergraduates as co-teacher of Human Sexuality, the largest class in the University. He is also co-author (with fellow psychiatrist Herant Katchadourian) of the best-selling textbook, *Fundamentals of Human Sexuality*. At the Stanford Law School, Dr. Lunde teaches a year-long seminar in advanced criminal law with Professor Anthony Amsterdam.

Dr. Lunde received his BA (1958) and MA (1964) degrees in psychology from Stanford, as well as his MD (1966). He then completed an internship in internal medicine and a residency in psychiatry at Stanford Medical Center and was appointed to the Medical School faculty in 1969.

From 1958 to 1960 he served as trial counsel for special courts-martial in the U.S. Navy. During 1960-61 he served as a member of a military court. He has served on the staffs of various county, VA, and state psychiatric hospitals, including California's Atascadero State Hospital for the criminally insane. Dr. Lunde has frequently been appointed to appear in state and federal courts as an expert witness in the field of forensic psychiatry. He is a member of the American Academy of Psychiatry and the Law. His many controversial cases include the Patricia Hearst trial, where he was one of three court-appointed psychiatrists to examine Ms. Hearst.

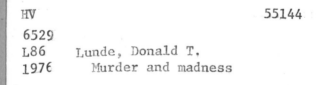